Better Homes & Gardens.

CHRISTMAS
FROM THE HEART.

Volume 29

Meredith Consumer Marketing
Des Moines, Iowa

CHRISTMAS
FROM THE HEART.

MEREDITH CORPORATION CONSUMER MARKETING
Director of Direct Marketing-Books: Daniel Fagan
Marketing Operations Manager: Max Daily
Assistant Marketing Manager: Kylie Dazzo
Content Manager: Julie Doll
Senior Production Manager: Liza Ward

WATERBURY PUBLICATIONS, INC.
Contributing Editor: Carol Field Dahlstrom
Contributing Copy Editor: Carrie Truesdell
Contributing Proofreader: Linda Wagner
Contributing Photographers: Jacob Fox, Marty Baldwin, Dera Burreson

Editorial Director: Lisa Kingsley
Creative Director: Ken Carlson
Associate Editor: Tricia Bergman
Associate Design Director: Doug Samuelson
Production Assistant: Mindy Samuelson

BETTER HOMES & GARDENS MAGAZINE
Editor in Chief: Stephen Orr
Executive Editor: Oma Blaise Ford
Managing Editor: Gregory H. Kayko
Creative Director: Jennifer D. Madara
Food Editor: Jan Miller

MEREDITH CORPORATION
President and CEO: Tom Harty
Chairman: Stephen M. Lacy

Contents

CHRISTMAS, HAPPY AND BRIGHT

Christmas really is the most wonderful time of the year! Colored lights shimmer in the windows, evergreens are adorned with sparkling trims, snow glistens in the countryside under clear, star-filled skies, and children's giggles can be heard everywhere as Christmas draws near. Almost like magic, the world becomes a happier and brighter place.

In this volume of *Christmas from the Heart,* we've given you clever do-it-yourself ideas and projects, decorating tips to deck the halls, easy gift wraps and handmade greeting cards, and delicious kitchen goodies to make your home reflect the season. Make your Christmas even sweeter with Red and Green Seven-Layer Bars or a clever Gingerbread Cookie Wreath. Make a double batch of Chocolate-Peppermint Filled Spritz to share with friends and neighbors. Having a holiday party? Stir up some Nacho Chicken Drummettes and Marinated Mozzarella with Basil. Serve with a glass of Sparkling Strawberry Mimosa for the perfect holiday appetizer.

The projects we share designed in classic Christmas red and white are sure to become favorites. Try your hand at making a Santa Pocket Stocking, a stunning poinsettia appliqué, Perched Paper Cardinals, and bakers twine trims. Love a country Christmas? Then you'll want to create our citrus-and-spice Christmas tree with gingerbread cookie ornaments and fragrant orange-slice trims. If you want to keep it simple this year, you'll really enjoy our chapter that shares dazzling last-minute centerpieces and decorating ideas that take only minutes to make. If you want soft and sweet, you'll fall in love with our personality-plus felt reindeer trims, our Cozy Sweater Snowman, and our beautiful Holly-Topped Trims. And for the kids, you'll love our Little Drummer Boy trims and Silly Reindeer Puppets.

As you prepare for the most wonderful time of the year, we hope these ideas and recipes will make your Christmas happy and bright as you create an unforgettable and beautiful *Christmas from the Heart.*

Merry Christmas!

Carol Field Dahlstrom

Holiday Classics...
Red, White, Christmas!

Bring the spirit of the season to your holiday home with classic decor in hues of delicious red and winter white.

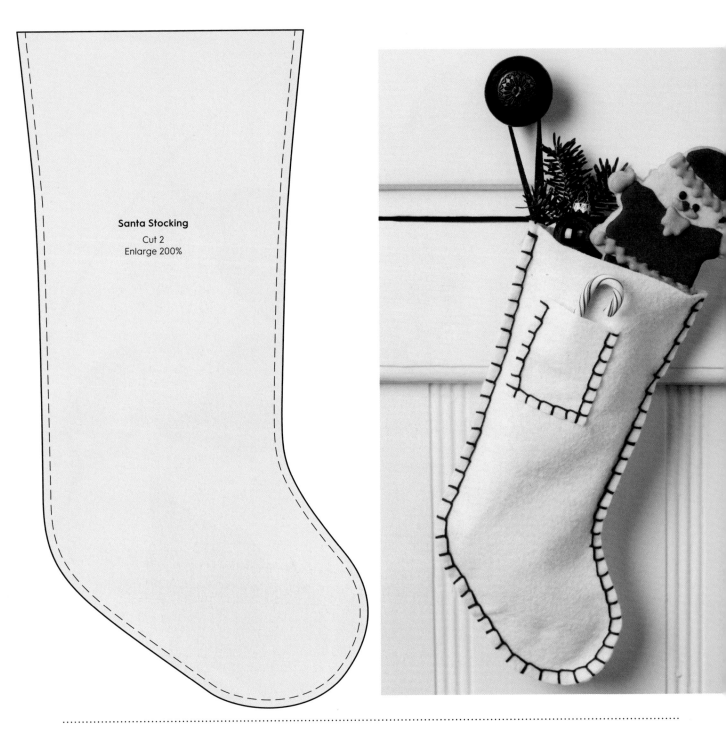

Santa Stocking
Cut 2
Enlarge 200%

SANTA POCKET STOCKING

Santa can stash a bounty of goodies inside this sweet stocking and add a special treat in the little pocket. Blanket-stitched edges are both functional and decorative for this delightful holiday stocking.

WHAT YOU NEED

⅝ yard white felt such as National Nonwovens • Scissors • Red embroidery floss • Embroidery needle • Sewing needle • White sewing thread • 10 inches of ½-inch-wide red grosgrain ribbon

WHAT YOU DO

1. Enlarge the stocking pattern, left, onto white paper; cut out. Fold felt in half and trace pattern onto doubled felt; cut out stocking through both layers. Cut out a 2×3-inch rectangle from felt for the pocket.

2. Use red embroidery floss and the Blanket Stitch to stitch around the pocket. Whipstitch the pocket to the front stocking piece leaving the top open. (See page 158 for Stitch Diagrams.)

3. Pin stocking pieces wrong sides together. Using six strands of embroidery floss and leaving top of stocking open, blanket-stitch stocking body pieces together. Sew ribbon in the corner of the stocking for a hanger.

OH CHRISTMAS TREE

Your holiday tree will sing with the spirit of the season when it is adorned with crimson cardinals, sparkling ribbon tassels, and Scandinavian-inspired folded white stars. Add some purchased red and white ball ornaments to continue the classic color theme. For instructions for the projects, see pages 12-14.

DRESSED-UP PACKAGES

Make a few extra bird and tassel ornaments to adorn those special gifts this year. Wrap your gift in red or white with a generous bow, and add a topper they will love to keep as an ornament.

PERCHED PAPER CARDINALS

Bright red scrapbook papers in Christmas prints and crimson shades make snow-dusted cardinals to rest on your holiday evergreen tree.

WHAT YOU NEED

Pencil • Scrapbook paper in prints and shades of red • Small scrap of yellow scrapbook paper • Scissors • Crafts glue • Scrapbooking adhesive spacers such as Pop Dots • Paintbrush • Fine glitter • Paper punch • Narrow ribbon

WHAT YOU DO

1. Trace the pattern, right, and cut out. Draw around the shapes on desired colors of scrapbook paper and cut out.
2. Place the pieces to form the bird. Use crafts glue to glue the bird together except for the wings. Place a spacer under the wings on both sides to secure the wings.
3. Very lightly use a paintbrush to brush the paper with glue where desired and dust with glitter. Punch a hole in the middle, top of the bird and add a ribbon for hanging.

Perched Paper Cardinal Patterns

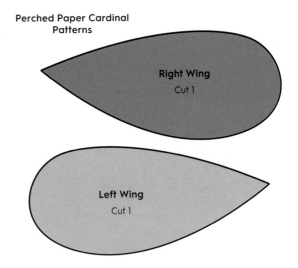

Right Wing
Cut 1

Left Wing
Cut 1

Belly
Cut 1

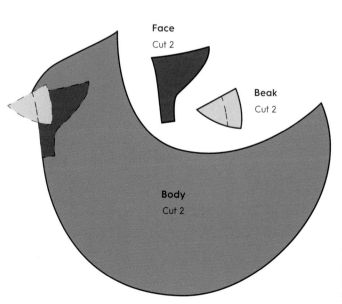

Face
Cut 2

Beak
Cut 2

Body
Cut 2

HOLIDAY RIBBON TASSELS

An assortment of red and white ribbons layer together to make a simple trim for your Christmas tree.

WHAT YOU NEED FOR ONE TASSEL
Eight 12-inch pieces of ribbon in desired colors • Red-and-white bakers twine • 10-inch piece of ribbon in desired color • Scissors

WHAT YOU DO
Lay the ribbons on a flat surface in the order you want to have them appear. Fold them over. Slide a piece of bakers twine through the loop. Take the 10-inch piece of ribbon and tie about 1 inch below the top. Make a double knot if necessary. Trim ends.

STAR PERFORMERS

Scandinavian and German holiday traditions embrace these intricate star motifs. Made with strips of bias tape or folded fabric, these sophisticated ornaments require just a series of folds and a little patience. Use winter white or any color that suits your fancy.

WHAT YOU NEED

1-inch-wide double-fold bias tape • Scissors • Embroidery floss or bakers twine • Needle

WHAT YOU DO

1. Cut four 12-inch bias tape strips. Fold each strip crosswise in half so one tail is about 1 inch longer than the other. Arrange the folded strips with the shorter lengths on top.

2. Holding one folded strip, thread both loose ends of a second strip through the loop of the first strip. Thread the loop of a third strip over the ends of the second strip. Thread the loop of the fourth strip over the ends of the third strip. Finally thread the loose ends of the fourth strip through the loop of the first strip. Pull all the loose ends gently to tighten the weaving into a box pattern (Photo 1).

3. Flip the assembly so the long pieces are on top. Fold the long end of one strip over the woven box. Moving in a circle, repeat with the remaining three long strips, folding each strip over the previous one. Pull the end of the last strip through the loop of the first strip (Photo 2). The strips should now all be about the same length. If the lengths are different, pull gently to adjust.

4. Fold the end of a strip to make a diagonal fold near the box. Flip the assembly and fold the end again to make a point (Photo 3). Fold the point in half. Tuck the tail into the center loop. Moving in a circle, repeat to make a folded

point for each end (Photo 4). Trim any extra bias tape ends if necessary. Press with a hot iron to set the folds.

5. Thread a length of embroidery floss onto a needle. Push the needle through an edge of the bias-tape star. Holding one loose end of floss, pull the length through the star. Remove floss from needle, and knot together ends to form a hanging loop.

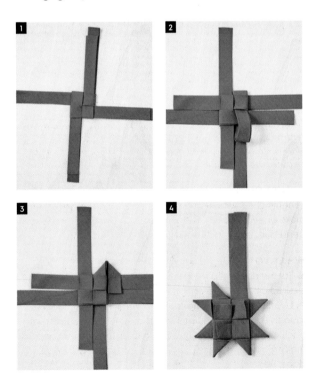

BERIBBONED GARLAND

Lengths of ribbon are tied onto golden cording to make a playful garland for your window, mantel, or door. Choose the kinds of ribbon that complement your holiday decorating theme.

WHAT YOU NEED

Lengths of ribbon about 18 inches long (we used about 20 to make one foot of garland) • Scissors • Cording in the length desired for finished garland plus 10 inches for tying

WHAT YOU DO

1. Cut the ribbons to the desired length. Lay them out in the desired order for the garland.
2. Lay the cording on the table. Fold the ribbon in half and loop over the cording leaving about 4 inches of cording at each end for hanging. Slip the two ends through the loop making a knot. Continue until desired length of garland is done. Rearrange and fluff the ribbons; trim the ends.

POINSETTIA-PRETTY APPLIQUÉ

Create the classic poinsettia motif using red cotton prints appliquéd on white linen for a stunning heirloom table piece to be cherished year after year.

FINISHED SIZE
18×13-inch oval

WHAT YOU NEED

FOR THE BACKGROUND
½ yard winter-white linen or cotton blend

FOR THE APPLIQUÉ
1 fat quarter each of 4 different red cotton prints varying in value or printed pattern

FOR THE FREEZER PAPER
22×17-inch rectangle

PAPER-BACKED FUSIBLE WEB
1 yard light-weight fusible web

BATTING
½ yard fusible fleece

BACKING FABRIC
½ yard red cotton

EMBELLISHMENTS
3 spools different colors of red rayon or polyester threads • Size No. 12 red cotton thread • Twelve ¼-inch to ⅜-inch pearl beads or white buttons

WHAT YOU DO

PREPARING BACKGROUND AND BINDING
1. Enlarge Poinsettia Oval Template, right, and following directions on template, trace oval on dull side of freezer paper. Cut out on traced line.
2. Open the folded pattern and place dull side up close to one end of the linen. Press in place. Cut out around the pattern, remove paper.
3. From the remainder of the linen, cut 60 inches total of 1½-inch wide bias strips.

PREPARING APPLIQUÉ
1. Using the Poinsettia Petal Appliqué Patterns on page 18, trace the number of pieces indicated on each petal on paper side of fusible web. (Patterns are already reversed.)
2. Number the red fabrics 1 to 4. Fuse petal patterns according to manufacturer's directions to the wrong side of the corresponding numbered fabrics. Cut out each piece on the traced line.

ARRANGING AND STITCHING APPLIQUÉ
1. Fuse the fleece to the back of the linen oval, following manufacturer's directions and pressing from the center to the edges. Cut fleece around the oval.
2. Remove the paper backing from each petal. Referring to the Poinsettia Placement Diagrams on page 18, arrange each poinsettia separately on a nonstick pressing sheet.
3. Position the poinsettias on the background with the petals at least ½ inch from the edge of the oval.

4. Using one of the red rayon threads and a satin or fine zigzag stitch (1 mm long and 1.75 mm wide), stitch around several of the petal pieces. Repeat using the other two colors to stitch around all of the petals.

FINISHING
1. Pin the backing cotton to the oval.
2. Quilt veins on each petal with the corresponding red thread.
3. Quilt straight lines in the background as if radiating from the center.
4. Cut the backing fabric to the edge of the oval making a very smooth edge.
5. Sew the three bias strips together to make a continuous binding. Stitch binding around the edge of the oval easing in around the curves (do not stretch the bias). Fold over and turn under ¼ inch. Whipstitch in place.
6. Using the No. 12 red cotton thread and a triple stitch, stitch in the ditch around the binding.
7. Sew the beads or buttons in the center of the flowers.
TIP: To ensure your surface for ironing is clean for working with a white background, place a piece of muslin or light fabric over your ironing board.

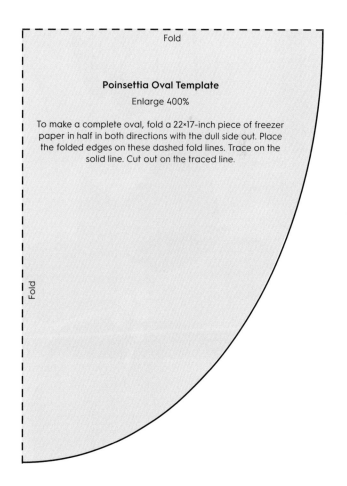

Fold

Poinsettia Oval Template

Enlarge 400%

To make a complete oval, fold a 22×17-inch piece of freezer paper in half in both directions with the dull side out. Place the folded edges on these dashed fold lines. Trace on the solid line. Cut out on the traced line.

Fold

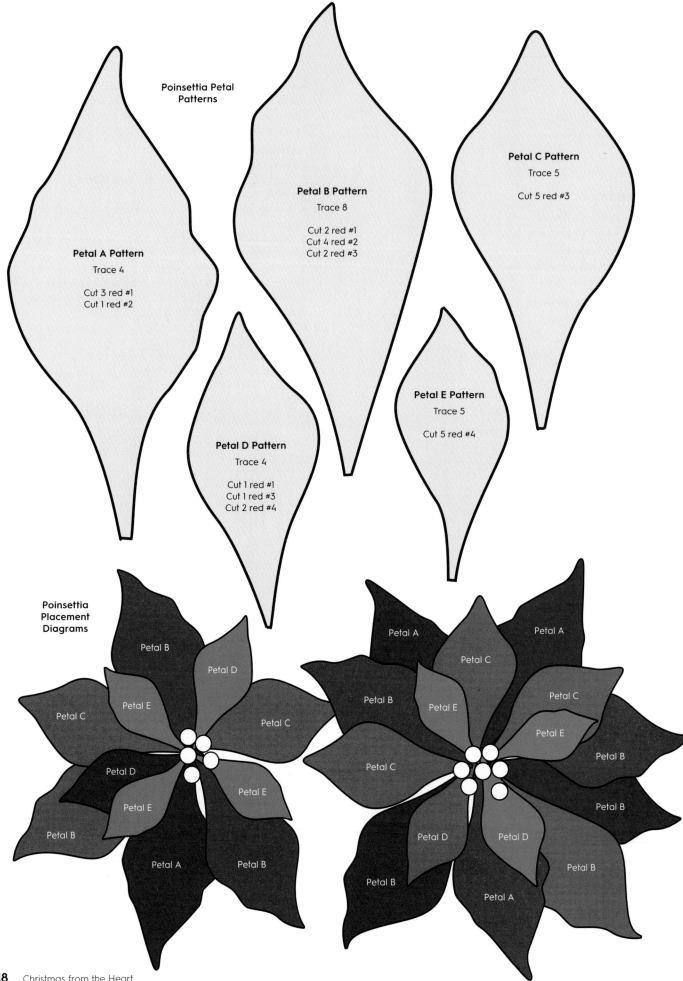

Poinsettia Petal Patterns

Petal A Pattern

Trace 4

Cut 3 red #1
Cut 1 red #2

Petal B Pattern

Trace 8

Cut 2 red #1
Cut 4 red #2
Cut 2 red #3

Petal C Pattern

Trace 5

Cut 5 red #3

Petal D Pattern

Trace 4

Cut 1 red #1
Cut 1 red #3
Cut 2 red #4

Petal E Pattern

Trace 5

Cut 5 red #4

Poinsettia Placement Diagrams

Petal B
Petal D
Petal E
Petal C
Petal C
Petal D
Petal E
Petal E
Petal B
Petal A
Petal B

Petal A
Petal A
Petal C
Petal B
Petal C
Petal E
Petal C
Petal E
Petal B
Petal B
Petal D
Petal D
Petal B
Petal B
Petal A

PEPPERMINT-STRIPED TRIMS

Cotton print fabric in a red-and-white stripe is the perfect covering for a simple-to-make holiday trim. Just pink the edges of the fabric, tuck a foam ball inside, and tie with ribbon.

WHAT YOU NEED

12×12-inch piece of red-and-white striped cotton fabric
• Pinking shears • 3-inch foam ball such as Styrofoam
• Rubber band • Red-and-white narrow ribbon • Straight pin • White grosgrain ribbon • Scissors • Holly sprig

WHAT YOU DO

1. Lay the fabric on a flat table; press if necessary. Use the pinking shears to trim around the edges of the fabric. Lay the foam ball in the middle of the fabric. Pull the fabric up and around the ball and secure with a rubber band. Adjust the folds of the fabric.

2. Pin the narrow ribbon inside the tucks for a hanger. Tie the grosgrain ribbon around the rubber band to conceal, tucking in a piece of greenery or holly sprig.

DRESSED-UP MANTEL

Your mantel can be decorated in no time with a few simple projects. Fresh or faux evergreen enjoys a lift with a few add-ons like eucalyptus and bright red berries. Wherever you live, you can enjoy the winter wonder of snowy branches when you choose flocked everlasting wreaths and garlands. Make the designs your own by adding berry picks and stems with leaves—such as fresh magnolia and boxwood—for a grand presentation. To make this woodland mantelscape, wrap and glue red and natural options on various-size papier-mâché cones.

SIMPLY-WRAPPED CONE TREE

Similar to the Wrapped Cone Ornament on page 22, simply wrap the cone and turn it upside down for a sweet setting of red and white trees. Make some using natural twine or solid-red twine as well.

HOLIDAY TWINERY

Nothing looks more festive than a tree and mantel decorated in crimson red and crisp white. Add in the deep green of fir or pine for a traditional Christmas-style palette. The handmade treasures on the tree share one readily available ingredient—bakers twine. Use it for stylish accents in every space. Whether you are a butcher, a baker, or a twine-tree maker, you'll be amazed at the array of colors this 12-ply cotton cord comes in.

WRAPPED CONE ORNAMENT

Each inverted cone holds a pretty berry-and-greens pick. Insert half a foam ball to hold the arrangement and add a loop hanger.

WHAT YOU NEED

7-inch papier-mâché cone • Crafts glue • 12-ply bakers twine in two colors • Scrapbook adhesive squares• 2-inch foam ball cut in half• Assorted berries and greens • Scissors

WHAT YOU DO

1. Poke a hole in the tip of cone. Add a bit of glue and push the end of bakers twine into the hole. Using glue or adhesive squares to secure placement, twirl and wrap the twine to cover the cone, leaving 1 inch at the top uncovered. Trim the twine and secure the end with glue.

2. Complete the wrap with a second color. Make a hanging loop by knotting the ends of a 9-inch length of twine. Glue it to the inside edge of the cone. Glue half a foam ball inside the cone and insert berry and greenery picks or stems.

COOKIE-CUTTER EASY

No two are alike, and each one is cuter than the next.

WHAT YOU NEED

Assorted cookie cutters • 12-ply red-and-white bakers twine • Scrapbook adhesive squares • Clear-drying crafts glue

WHAT YOU DO

1. Make a hanging loop by knotting a 6-inch tail on the beginning end of the twine. Knot the loop around the top of the cookie cutter.

2. Wrap twine to cover the entire shape, using small adhesive squares to hold twine in place while you wrap. To finish, tuck in the cut ends and use a dot of glue to secure.

TIP: Estimate how much twine you'll need to cover your cookie cutter. Cut that length and wrap it into a small ball. If you run short, add more by tying ends together.

TWINE-WRAPPED BALLS

A simple ball shape becomes a colorful Christmas trim with a simple bakers twine and a wooden bead.

WHAT YOU NEED

12-ply red-and-white bakers twine • ½-inch wooden bead • Hot-glue gun and glue sticks• 2½-inch papier-mâché ball ornament • Paint brush • Clear-drying crafts glue • Yarn needle • Scissors

WHAT YOU DO

1. With a length of twine, make a loop, thread through bead, and knot loose ends. Trim and hot-glue knotted end into ornament hanging hole at top of ball.

2. Using a small brush and crafts glue, coat the top part of the papier-mâché ball, and wind twine around ball to cover glue. Brush on more glue and continue to wrap until the ball is almost covered. Using a yarn needle, poke a small hole in the bottom. Add a dot of hot glue and insert the end of twine into hole.

GIFTS OF JOY

Purchased tags become personalized when you spell out a greeting or holiday motif with bakers twine.

WHAT YOU NEED

Precut chipboard or cardstock tags • Small-hole punch
• 12-ply red-and-white bakers twine • Yarn needle
• Crafts glue

WHAT YOU DO

1. If using chipboard, lightly pencil a word in script or holiday motif. Use a small-hole punch to make a hole at the beginning; push the twine end to the back and dot with glue to secure. Working along the letters, glue the twine to finish the word. Punch a hole at the end. Trim and push twine through; glue to back.

2. For cardstock, draw design with a pencil. Use a small-hole punch or push through with a nail. Secure one twine end on the back with a dot of glue. Use yarn needle to sew in and out of the holes to create the shape, and secure end to the back with a dot of glue.

WRAPPED AND READY

Gift wrapping is easy when you stick to a limited palette of white, red, and kraft paper. Employ materials in a variety of textures, such as glossy and matte papers, sleek and rough ribbons (think satin and raffia), and twine. You also can use solid-color purchased boxes to make the job even easier. Simply add ribbons, twine, and tags to give the gift the personality you want. When using bakers twine, try using 3 or 4 strands at a time to make the area appear thicker. To crisscross twine or ribbon, lay the wrapped box right side up and then wrap, cross, and turn. That way your bow will appear on the front side of the box when you are done. Add a handmade gift tag.

DECK THE HALLS

String the cranberries then wire in pinecones for woodland swags that will bring fa-la-las to the decoration of cabinet fronts, doorways, and windows. For an extra holiday note, bring out red-and-white transferware china pieces to lend their merry measure.

RED-AND-WHITE TASSEL GARLAND

Simple bakers twine becomes a festive tassel garland with the addition of a few wood and wool beads.

WHAT YOU NEED

Red-and-white bakers twine • Scissors • 2×3-inch piece of sturdy cardboard • Wool beads • Wood beads • Needle

WHAT YOU DO

1. Wrap bakers twine around the cardboard until you have the desired tassel thickness, about 50 times. Gently slide the loop off of the cardboard.

2. Cut a piece of bakers twine 5 inches long and wrap around the top of the tassel, about a ½ inch down from the top, several times, securing with a knot. Cut off loose ends. On the bottom of the tassel, cut the loop.

3. Trim the tassel to desired length. Using a needle, thread the tassels, wool beads and wood beads onto garland.

HOW TO MAKE A TASSEL

1. Wrap yarn many times around cardboard. Tie into a bundle at one end; cut other end (A).

2. Wrap yarn around the bundle several times near the tied end; tie in place (B).

3. Trim the loose ends of the yarn to the desired tassel length (C).

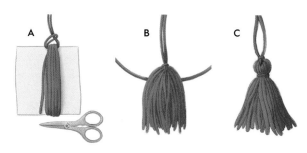

A   B   C

SANTA'S DOWNHILL FUN

Santa is set for a wild ride down a snowy slope. Paint his easy-to-assemble wood figure, and then accessorize with packages, a tiny deer, and just a little glitter. Don't forget felt scarves to keep Santa and his friend warm on their chilly jaunt.

WHAT YOU NEED

Two 1³⁄₁₆-inch-long wood ladybug splits (mittens), see Sources, page 160 • Two 1-inch-long wood ladybug splits (shoes), see Sources, page 160 • Small drill with small drill bits • Two bamboo skewers • 1¾×1-inch wood egg (head) • Glue: wood, fabric, crafts • 2-inch wood ball with one flat edge (body) • Assorted artists brushes • Acrylic paint: red, burgundy, black, desired flesh color, cream, pink, green • Five ¼-inch pom-poms: white • Fine-tip permanent marking pens: black and brown • Red color pencil • Clear acrylic spray finish: matte • Clear glitter • Miniature knit hat: red • Chenille stems: white and bumpy red • 2½×6-inch wood sled • Hot-glue gun and glue sticks • Miniature deer figurine • Wood cubes: two ½ inch, one ¾ inch • Two ¾-inch-diameter snowflake sequins • Mica flakes • 1×6-inch felted wool strip (Santa's scarf) • ½×5-inch felted wool strip (deer's scarf) • Mini bottle-brush tree

WHAT YOU DO

ASSEMBLING THE BODY

1. Using a drill bit slightly larger than the diameter of a bamboo skewer, drill a hole into the smaller portion of each of the four ladybug splits (mittens and shoes). Using wood glue, adhere 2-inch lengths of bamboo skewer into holes in shoes to make legs; let dry.

2. Drill a hole at an angle into back of wood egg (head). Note: Angle should allow small end of head to point downward when bamboo skewer is inserted. Dab wood glue onto one end of a bamboo skewer and push the glued end into the hole; let dry.

3. Drill hole into flat edge of wood ball (body). Paint body red; let dry. Referring to photos, below, drill two holes for legs approximately ¼ inch from flat edge and ¼ inch apart.

4. Paint legs red with burgundy stripes. Paint shoes black. Let dry. Dab wood glue on ends of legs and insert into body.

5. Drill a hole into the top of body (for neck). Trim bamboo skewer attached to head to about ¾ inch. Dab glue on skewer end and insert it into top of body, leaving about ½ inch of skewer exposed between the body and head; let dry.

PAINTING THE FACE

1. Paint head and neck flesh color. Paint a cream beard. Let dry. Using fabric glue, adhere a pom-pom for the nose. Paint nose pink or flesh color. Draw eyes using black fine-tip marker. Draw an O-shape mouth using brown fine-tip marker. Paint cream highlights on eyes. Add red circles for cheeks using color pencil. Spray figure using matte clear acrylic spray; let dry.

2. Brush crafts glue on beard. Sprinkle clear glitter onto wet glue. Use fabric glue to attach knit hat to head. Using fabric glue, attach a 6½-inch white chenille stem around bottom of body for coat trim.

FINISHING THE FIGURE

1. Drill a hole through the sled approximately 1½ inches from the center front. Dab wood glue onto a ½-inch bamboo skewer to attach seated Santa to sled. Hot-glue deer to sled behind Santa. Paint wood cubes green, red, and/or other colors to make presents; let dry. Hot-glue stack of presents to sled behind the deer. Hot-glue snowflake sequins to tops of presents for bows.

2. Using fabric glue, attach two pom-poms to front of Santa's body and one to each shoe near the leg. Brush all pom-poms and hat brim using cream paint. Brush crafts glue onto top of sled. Sprinkle mica flakes onto wet glue; let dry. Brush crafts glue onto pom-poms and hat brim. Sprinkle mica flakes. Brush crafts glue on reindeer back and sprinkle with mica flakes. Let dry.

3. Paint mittens green; let dry. Fold a 6-inch length of bumpy red chenille stem in half. Place chenille stem across the neck with the fold under the chin. Dab fabric glue on front and back of neck and crisscross the chenille stem behind the neck to form an arm at each side. Tie a 1×6-inch felted wool strip around Santa's neck for a scarf. Fringe scarf ends with scissors. Tie ½×5-inch felted wool strip around deer's neck and fringe. Attach mittens to arms and glue to sled handle. Glue small bottle-brush tree into one arm.

HOOPS OF JOY

Spread a holiday sentiment with an ornament that spells it out. For decorative impact, thick off-white stitching fills in the lettering on a red cotton background. If your holiday decor is less traditional, select a background color to match your look. Make the ornament in multiples. Trace as many designs as you need—then stitch at your leisure.

WHAT YOU NEED

7-inch square of red cotton fabric • White chalk pencil • 3-inch round wood embroidery hoop • Ecru embroidery floss • Embroidery needle • Crafts glue • 7 inches of ecru twill tape

WHAT YOU DO

1. Using a light box or sunny window and a white chalk pencil, trace the pattern, right, in the center of the red fabric square. Center design in embroidery hoop, pulling fabric taut; tighten screw.

2. Using six strands of ecru embroidery floss, use closely spaced, staggered Straight Stitches to fill in the heavy strokes of each letter. Backstitch the light strokes of the letters. (See page 158 for Stitch Diagrams.)

3. Remove fabric from hoop. Using a warm dry iron and working on wrong side, press finished embroidery. Insert embroidery back into hoop, centering design and pulling fabric taut; tighten screw.

4. Trim fabric 2 inches beyond hoop edge. Wrap and glue the fabric to the back side of the hoop; let dry. Trim excess fabric as needed. Tie twill tape around screw to form a hanging loop.

Joy Lettering Pattern

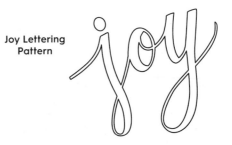

MERRILY MADE

Inexpensive ornaments get a luxe, lovely look thanks to a surprisingly easy technique. Simply swirl paints for finished orbs that mimic marbling. You can use red paint, shown here, for a classic Christmas look, or bling it up with gold or silver paint instead. A wreath of lamb's ears, velvet leaves, and sprigs of millinery berries adds fullness, texture, and color.

WHAT YOU NEED

About 30 acrylic ornaments (ours are 67 mm) • assorted crafts paint colors • Plastic cups • Wire wreath form • Lamb's ears garland • Florists wire • Velvet millinery leaves • Millinery berries • Hot-glue gun and glue sticks

WHAT YOU DO

1. Remove hangers from all ornaments. Dilute paints to a 3:1 paint-to-water ratio. Pour two or three colors into each ornament and swirl around to create marbling pattern. See Photos 1 and 2.

2. Place ornament upside down on a cup. Let dry for several days. **Tip:** Marble ornaments a week before assembling the wreath.

3. Wrap garland around wreath form and attach using florists wire. To attach ornaments, hook each wire ornament hanger to the wreath frame, place the hanger cap onto the hanger, and add the ornament. Repeat, working your way around the wreath until full. Place millinery leaves and berries intermittently around the wreath, securing with hot glue.

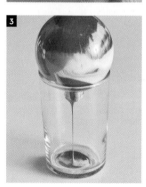

Sweet Holiday Favorites

The best holiday traditions come from the kitchen.
Let this collection of luscious pies, cakes, cookies,
and hot drinks inspire you this season.

CHOCOLATE CHUNK AND CARAMEL PECAN PIE

This decadent pie is filled with homemade caramel sauce, rich dark chocolate, and buttery pecans, then finished with a sprinkle of crunchy sea salt for the perfect holiday dessert.

WHAT YOU NEED
½   cup butter
¾   cup light-color corn syrup
⅔   cup granulated sugar
⅔   cup packed brown sugar
2   Tbsp. bourbon or water
½   tsp. fleur de sel or other fine sea salt
1   cup heavy cream
2   tsp. vanilla
1   recipe Pastry for Single-Crust Pie (page 33)
3   eggs, lightly beaten
2½   cups pecan halves
6   oz. dark, bittersweet, or semisweet chocolate, chopped
     Fleur de sel or other fine sea salt

WHAT YOU DO
1. For caramel sauce, in a medium saucepan heat butter over low heat until melted, stirring frequently. Stir in corn syrup, granulated sugar, brown sugar, bourbon, and ½ tsp. fleur de sel. Bring to boiling over medium heat, stirring constantly; reduce heat. Boil gently, uncovered, 30 minutes or until reduced to 1¾ cups, stirring frequently. Remove from heat. Carefully whisk in heavy cream and vanilla. Cool 30 minutes.

2. Meanwhile, preheat oven to 350°F. Prepare Pastry for Single-Crust Pie. On a lightly floured surface, use your hands to slightly flatten dough. Roll pastry into a 12-inch circle. Transfer pastry to a 9-inch pie plate, being careful not to stretch pastry. Trim pastry to ½ inch beyond edge of plate; crimp edge as desired.

3. For filling, transfer 1¼ cups of the caramel sauce to a large bowl. Stir in eggs until combined. Stir in pecans and chocolate. Pour filling into pastry shell. Cover edge of pie with foil to prevent overbrowning. Bake 25 minutes. Remove foil. Bake 20 minutes more or until filling is set. Cool on a wire rack.

4. To serve, reheat the remaining caramel sauce over low heat. Spoon some of the warm sauce over pie. Sprinkle lightly with additional fleur de sel. If desired, serve with remaining sauce. Makes 10 servings.

Tip Store leftover caramel sauce in an airtight container in the refrigerator up to 5 days. To serve, heat over low heat until warm. Serve over ice cream or desserts.

DUTCH APPLE PIE

Some Dutch apple pies are topped with a lattice-style crust, and others call for a deep-dish pie plate. This recipe includes a deliciously crumbly streusel topping. Gild the lily with a scoop of ice cream. (Pictured on page 30.)

WHAT YOU NEED
1   recipe Pastry for Single-Crust Pie (page 33)
1½   cups all-purpose flour
½   cup packed brown sugar
½   tsp. salt
1   tsp. ground cinnamon
¾   cup butter, cut up
½   cup chopped walnuts
¾   cup granulated sugar
2   Tbsp. all-purpose flour
6   cups thinly sliced, peeled apples
¼   cup heavy cream

WHAT YOU DO
1. Preheat oven to 450°F. Prepare Pastry for Single-Crust Pie. On a lightly floured surface use your hands to slightly flatten pastry ball. Roll pastry into a 12-inch circle. Line a 9-inch pie plate with pastry circle. Trim and flute edge.

2. For streusel, in a large bowl combine the 1½ cups flour, the brown sugar, salt, and ½ tsp. of the cinnamon. Cut in butter until mixture resembles coarse crumbs. Stir in walnuts.

3. For filling, in an extra-large bowl combine granulated sugar, the 2 Tbsp. flour, and the remaining ½ tsp. cinnamon. Add apples; toss to coat. Transfer to the pastry-lined pie plate. Carefully drizzle with cream. Mound streusel over filling, patting down and completely covering filling.

4. Place a foil-lined baking sheet on rack below pie. Bake 15 minutes. Reduce oven temperature to 375°F. Bake 50 to 60 minutes more or until filling is bubbly. Cover pie loosely with foil after 30 minutes of baking. Cool on a wire rack. Makes 8 servings.

Pastry for Single-Crust Pie In a medium bowl stir together 1½ cups all-purpose flour and ½ tsp. salt. Using a pastry blender, cut in ¼ cup shortening and ¼ cup butter, cut up, or shortening until pea size. Sprinkle 1 Tbsp. ice water over part of the flour mixture; toss with a fork. Push moistened pastry to side of bowl. Repeat moistening flour mixture with ice water, 1 Tbsp. at a time, until all of the flour mixture is moistened (¼ to ⅓ cup cold water total). Gather pastry into a ball, kneading gently until it comes together.

PUMPKIN CAKE ROLL

A cake roll never fails to impress. Here, a layer of spiced pumpkin cake and a sweet, cream cheese and butter filling create a festive dessert the whole family will love.

WHAT YOU NEED
- ¾ cup all-purpose flour
- 2 tsp. ground cinnamon
- 1 tsp. baking powder
- 1 tsp. ground ginger
- ½ tsp. salt
- ½ tsp. ground nutmeg
- 3 eggs, room temperature
- 1 cup granulated sugar
- ⅔ cup canned pumpkin
- 1 tsp. lemon juice
- 1 cup finely chopped walnuts

- Powdered sugar
- 1 8-oz. pkg. cream cheese, softened
- ⅓ cup butter, softened
- 1½ tsp. vanilla
- 1½ cups powdered sugar

WHAT YOU DO
1. Preheat oven to 375°F. Grease a 15×10-inch baking pan. Line bottom with waxed paper or parchment paper; grease paper. In a small bowl stir together first six ingredients (through nutmeg).

2. In a large bowl beat eggs with a mixer on high 5 minutes or until thick and lemon color. Gradually add granulated sugar, beating on medium until light and fluffy. Stir in pumpkin and lemon juice. Beat in flour mixture on low to medium just until combined. Spread batter in prepared pan. Sprinkle with walnuts.

3. Bake 15 minutes or until cake springs back when lightly touched. Immediately loosen edges of cake from pan and turn out onto a towel sprinkled with powdered sugar; remove paper. Roll towel and cake into a spiral, starting from a short side. Cool on a wire rack.

4. Meanwhile, for filling, in a medium bowl beat cream cheese, butter, and vanilla on medium until smooth. Gradually beat in the 1½ cups powdered sugar.

5. Unroll cake; remove towel. Spread cake with filling to within 1 inch of the edges. Roll up cake; trim ends. Cover and chill 2 to 48 hours. Makes 8 servings.

ginger, cinnamon, baking powder, baking soda, salt, nutmeg, and cardamom; set aside.

2. In a large bowl beat butter with a mixer on medium to high 30 seconds. Add brown sugar. Beat until light and fluffy, scraping side of bowl occasionally. Add eggs, one at a time, beating well after each addition. Stir in molasses and grated ginger. Alternately add flour mixture and beer in three additions, beating on medium just until combined after each addition. Pour batter into the prepared pan.

3. Bake 40 to 50 minutes or until a wooden toothpick inserted near the center comes out clean. Cool in pan on a wire rack for 10 minutes. Remove cake from pan. Sprinkle with powdered sugar. Serve warm with *Lemony Hard Sauce.* Makes 12 servings.

Lemony Hard Sauce In a medium bowl beat ¼ cup butter, softened, with a mixer on medium to high until light and fluffy. Beat in ¾ cup powdered sugar, 2 Tbsp. lemon or orange liqueur, 2 tsp. lemon or orange zest, and 1 tsp. vanilla until smooth.

RED AND GREEN SEVEN-LAYER BARS

This seven-layer bar recipe has all kinds of tasty ingredients, like chocolate chip cookie dough, flaked coconut, white baking pieces, and red and green milk chocolate pieces, and will make a luscious addition to a cookie plate to share with neighbors and friends.

WHAT YOU NEED

1	16.5-oz. roll refrigerated chocolate chip cookie dough
6	oz. white baking chocolate, chopped, or 1 cup white baking chips
1	cup butterscotch-flavor chips
1	cup lightly salted roasted cashew pieces, cocktail peanuts, or salted mixed nuts, coarsely chopped
1	14-oz. can sweetened condensed milk
1	cup red and green candy-coated milk chocolate pieces
1⅓	cups flaked or shredded coconut

WHAT YOU DO

1. Preheat oven to 350°F. Line a 13×9-inch baking pan with foil, extending foil over edges. Lightly grease foil. For crust, cut cookie dough into ½-inch slices. Press into prepared pan, covering bottom completely. Bake 5 minutes. Remove from oven.

2. Top crust with remaining ingredients in order listed: white chocolate, butterscotch chips, cashews, sweetened condensed milk, candy-coated chocolate pieces, and coconut. Press down firmly with the back of a spoon.

3. Bake 25 minutes or until edges are lightly browned. Cool in pan on a wire rack. Using foil, lift out uncut cookies. Cut into bars. Makes 30 servings.

To Store Place bars in a single layer in an airtight container. Store in refrigerator up to 3 days or freeze up to 3 months.

STOUT GINGERBREAD WITH LEMONY HARD SAUCE

Buttery lemon sauce spooned over slices of moist, fragrant gingerbread is a classic holiday dessert. Stout beer adds richness and underscores the spices.

WHAT YOU NEED

	Nonstick spray for baking
¾	cup stout beer (such as Guinness)
2½	cups all-purpose flour
1	Tbsp. ground ginger
2	tsp. ground cinnamon
1½	tsp. baking powder
½	tsp. baking soda
½	tsp. salt
¼	tsp. freshly grated nutmeg or ⅛ tsp. ground nutmeg
¼	tsp. ground cardamom
1	cup butter, softened
1¼	cups packed brown sugar
3	eggs
1	cup mild-flavor molasses
1	Tbsp. grated fresh ginger
1	Tbsp. powdered sugar
1	recipe Lemony Hard Sauce

WHAT YOU DO

1. Preheat oven to 350°F. Generously coat a 10-inch fluted tube pan with nonstick spray for baking. Pour beer into a measuring cup and let stand at room temperature 15 minutes. In a medium bowl stir together flour, ground

2. Fit a cookie press with a rosette plate. Force unchilled dough through cookie press 1 inch apart onto ungreased cookie sheets. If desired, sprinkle half of the cookies with red sprinkles. Bake 8 to 10 minutes or until edges are firm but not brown. Remove; cool on wire racks.

3. Spread bottoms of half of the cookies with Chocolate-Peppermint Filling. Top with remaining cookies. Makes 48 servings.

Chocolate Peppermint Filling In a large bowl beat ¼ cup softened butter with a mixer on medium 30 seconds. Beat in 1 cup powdered sugar and ⅓ cup unsweetened cocoa powder. Beat in 3 Tbsp. milk, 1 tsp. vanilla, and ¼ tsp. peppermint extract until combined. Beat in 1½ cups powdered sugar until fluffy. If necessary, beat in 1 to 2 Tbsp. additional milk to make filling spreadable.

COCOA MASCARPONE CUTOUTS

Use the basic cookie cutter shapes you already have on hand to create jolly Santas with a little help from icing, frosting, and sprinkles.

WHAT YOU NEED
- ½ cup butter, softened
- ½ cup mascarpone cheese or 4 oz. cream cheese, softened
- 1 cup sugar
- 1 tsp. baking powder
- ¼ tsp. baking soda
- ¼ tsp. salt
- 1½ tsp. vanilla
- 1 egg
- ¼ cup unsweetened cocoa powder
- 2¼ cups all-purpose flour
- 1 recipe Royal Icing (optional)
- 1 recipe Buttercream Frosting (optional)

WHAT YOU DO

1. In a large bowl beat butter and mascarpone cheese with a mixer on medium 30 seconds. Add next four ingredients (through salt); beat until combined, scraping bowl as needed. Beat in vanilla and egg. Beat in cocoa powder and as much flour as you can with the mixer. Stir in any remaining flour. Divide dough in half. Cover and chill 30 to 60 minutes or until dough is easy to handle.

2. Preheat oven to 375°F. On a lightly floured surface, roll one portion of dough at a time to ⅛ inch thick. Using a 2½- to 3-inch cookie cutter, cut dough into desired shapes. Place 2 inches apart on an ungreased cookie sheet. Reroll scraps as needed.

3. Bake 5 to 6 minutes or until edges are set. Cool on cookie sheet 1 minute. Remove; cool on a wire rack. Decorate as desired with Royal Icing and/or Buttercream Frosting. Makes 32 servings.

CHOCOLATE-PEPPERMINT FILLED SPRITZ

Avoid chilling the dough for these chocolate-peppermint sandwich cookies. You want the dough to be soft enough to press out. Sprinkle with colored sugar before baking if you'd like.

WHAT YOU NEED
- 1½ cups butter, softened
- 1 cup granulated sugar
- 1 tsp. baking powder
- ¼ tsp. baking soda
- ¼ cup plain Greek yogurt
- 1 egg
- 1 tsp. vanilla
- ¼ tsp. peppermint extract
- 3½ cups all-purpose flour
- 1 recipe Chocolate Peppermint Filling
  Red sprinkles (optional)

WHAT YOU DO

1. Preheat oven to 375°F. In a large bowl beat butter with a mixer on medium to high 30 seconds. Add sugar, baking powder, and baking soda. Beat until combined, scraping bowl as needed. Beat in yogurt, egg, vanilla, and peppermint extract. Beat in as much of the flour as you can with the mixer. Stir in any remaining flour.

ROYAL ICING

WHAT YOU NEED
1   16-oz. pkg. powdered sugar (4 cups)
3   Tbsp. meringue powder*
½   tsp. cream of tartar
½   cup warm water
1   tsp. vanilla

WHAT YOU DO
In a large bowl stir together powdered sugar, meringue powder, and cream of tartar. Add the water and vanilla. Beat with a mixer on low until combined. Beat on high 7 to 10 minutes or until icing is very stiff. If needed, beat in additional water to reach desired consistency for piping or "flooding". (When not using icing, keep it covered with plastic wrap or a damp paper towel to prevent drying out.) If desired, chill up to 48 hours. Stir before using.
* Look for meringue powder in hobby stores or where cake decorating supplies are sold.

BUTTERCREAM FROSTING

WHAT YOU NEED
½   cup butter, softened
2   cups powdered sugar
1   Tbsp. plus 2 tsp. heavy cream
½   tsp. clear vanilla

WHAT YOU DO
In a large bowl beat butter with a mixer on medium 1 to 2 minutes or until creamy. Beat in ½ cup of the powdered sugar. Add 1 Tbsp. of the cream, and the vanilla; beat on low until combined. Gradually beat in remaining 1½ cups powdered sugar just until combined. Beat on medium 5 minutes or until fluffy, scraping bowl as needed. Add remaining 2 tsp. cream; beat on high 1 minute more.

GINGERBREAD COOKIE WREATH

Gather 'round to share this Christmas wreath craft that's meant to be eaten, too. Decorate with royal icing, edible glitter, and white sugar pearls.

WHAT YOU NEED

½   cup shortening
¼   cup butter, softened
½   cup granulated sugar
1   tsp. baking powder
1   tsp. ground ginger
½   tsp. baking soda
½   tsp. ground cinnamon
½   tsp. ground cloves
¼   tsp. salt
1   egg
½   cup molasses
1   Tbsp. cider vinegar
3   cups all-purpose flour
1   recipe Royal Icing (page 37)

WHAT YOU DO

1. In a large bowl beat shortening and butter with a mixer on medium to high 30 seconds. Add sugar, baking powder, ginger, baking soda, cinnamon, cloves, and salt. Beat until combined, scraping bowl as needed. Beat in egg, molasses, and vinegar. Beat in as much of the flour as you can with the mixer. Stir in any remaining flour. Divide dough in half. Cover and chill 1 hour or until dough is easy to handle.

2. Preheat oven to 375°F. Trace a 10-inch circle on two pieces of parchment paper; turn papers over onto two cookie sheets. On a lightly floured surface, roll one portion of dough to ¼ inch thick. Using a 3- to 4-inch snowflake- or star-shape cutter, cut out dough. Arrange cutouts on one parchment-lined sheet, using circle as a guide and overlapping edges of cutouts slightly. Reroll scraps as needed. Repeat with remaining portion of dough to make a second wreath.

3. Bake 9 to 11 minutes or until edges are firm. Cool on cookie sheet. Decorate wreaths as desired with Royal Icing. Makes 36 servings.

COCONUT-MACADAMIA BARK

Give your bark dessert a tropical twist with this tasty coconut bark creation. Kids will enjoy helping make this quick and easy treat.

WHAT YOU NEED

6   oz. vanilla-flavor candy coating, chopped (1 cup)
6   oz. white baking chocolate, chopped (1 cup)
1   Tbsp. shortening
1½ cups macadamia nuts, chopped
1½ tsp. finely shredded lime peel
¾   cup flaked coconut, toasted*
    Lime zest (optional)

WHAT YOU DO

1. Line a large baking sheet with heavy foil; grease foil.
2. In a large microwave-safe bowl combine candy coating, white chocolate, and shortening. Microwave, uncovered, on high 1½ to 2 minutes or until chocolate melts, stirring every 30 seconds. Stir in nuts and lime peel. Pour chocolate mixture onto the prepared baking sheet. Spread mixture evenly in a layer about ¼ inch thick. Sprinkle with coconut and, if desired, additional lime zest; lightly press into chocolate mixture.
3. Chill candy 30 minutes or until firm. Use foil to lift candy. Cut or break into pieces. Makes 20 servings.
*Tip To toast coconut, spread it in an even layer in a shallow baking pan. Bake in a 350°F oven 5 to 10 minutes, shaking pan once or twice. Watch closely as coconut can burn quickly.

MARCONA ALMOND TOFFEE

Buttery thick toffee gets a layer of white chocolate and salted nuts for the perfect crunch. Marcona almonds are a type of almond from Spain, and their texture is closer to that of a macadamia nut.

WHAT YOU NEED

    Nonstick cooking spray
2   cups butter
2   cups sugar
1   tsp. salt
1   tsp. vanilla
1   cup chopped white baking chocolate (6 oz.)
1   tsp. shortening
1   cup roasted and salted Marcona almonds

WHAT YOU DO

1. Line a 15×10-inch baking pan with foil; coat foil with cooking spray.
2. In a large saucepan combine butter, sugar, and salt. Stir over medium heat until the sugar has completely melted and mixture boils. Clip a candy thermometer to the pan and continue stirring over medium heat until mixture reaches 290°F, about 15 minutes. Remove from heat and stir in vanilla.
3. Pour the toffee into the prepared pan, tipping pan to evenly spread. Allow to cool on a wire rack. In a small saucepan melt white baking chocolate and shortening. Spread melted chocolate over toffee and sprinkle with almonds. Chill at least 30 minutes or until chocolate is set. Break into pieces. Makes 24 servings.

CARAMELS

Soft and chewy, these salted caramels will melt in your mouth. Before you begin, make sure you have a candy thermometer on hand.

WHAT YOU NEED

- 1   cup chopped walnuts, toasted if desired (optional)
- 1   cup butter
- 2¼ cups packed brown sugar
- 2   cups half-and-half or light cream
- 1   cup light-color corn syrup
- 1   tsp. vanilla
       Fleur de sel or other flaked sea salt

WHAT YOU DO

1. Line an 8-inch or 9-inch square baking pan with foil, extending foil over edges of pan. Butter foil. If desired, sprinkle walnuts over bottom of pan.

2. In a 3-qt. heavy saucepan melt butter over low heat. Add brown sugar, half-and-half, and corn syrup; mix well. Cook and stir over medium-high heat until mixture boils. Clip a candy thermometer to the side of the pan. Reduce heat to medium; continue boiling at a moderate, steady rate, stirring frequently, until the thermometer registers 248°F, firm-ball stage (45 to 60 minutes). Adjust heat as necessary to maintain a steady boil, and watch temperature carefully during the last 10 to 15 minutes of cooking as temperature can increase quickly at the end.

3. Remove saucepan from heat; remove thermometer. Stir in vanilla. Quickly pour mixture into prepared pan. Let stand about 2 hours or until firm. When firm, use foil to lift it out of pan. Use a buttered knife to cut into 1-inch squares. Lightly sprinkle with fleur de sel. Wrap each piece in waxed paper or plastic wrap. Store at room temperature up to 2 weeks. Makes 64 servings.

Shortcut Caramels Prepare as directed, except substitute one 14-oz. can (1¼ cups) sweetened condensed milk for the half-and-half. Bring mixture to boiling over medium heat instead of medium-high heat. This mixture will take less time to reach 248°F (about 20 to 25 minutes instead of 45 to 60 minutes).

HOMEMADE MARSHMALLOWS

If you've never tried homemade marshmallows, you're in for a treat! And if you have, you know why they're worth the effort: They're light, airy, fluffy, and rife with fresh vanilla flavor that most store-bought marshmallows simply cannot match.

WHAT YOU NEED

	Nonstick cooking spray
2	envelopes unflavored gelatin (4¼ tsp.)
¾	cup cold water
2	cups granulated sugar
⅔	cup light-color corn syrup
⅓	cup refrigerated egg white product* or 2 pasteurized liquid egg whites
1	Tbsp. vanilla
¼	tsp. salt
⅔	cup powdered sugar
3	Tbsp. cornstarch
	Cocoa powder or gold luster dust (optional)

WHAT YOU DO

1. Line a 13×9-inch baking pan with plastic wrap or line bottom of pan with waxed paper or parchment paper. Coat the plastic or paper with nonstick cooking spray.

2. In a large metal or heatproof bowl sprinkle gelatin over ½ cup of the cold water; set aside.

3. In a 2-qt. heavy saucepan stir together remaining ¼ cup water, 1¾ cups of the sugar, and the corn syrup until combined. Bring to boiling over medium-high heat. Clip a candy thermometer to the side of the saucepan. Cook, without stirring, over medium-high heat until thermometer registers 260°F, hard-ball stage (12 to 15 minutes). Remove from heat; pour over gelatin mixture in bowl and stir well to combine (mixture will foam and bubble up in the bowl).

4. Meanwhile, in a clean large mixing bowl beat egg whites, vanilla, and salt with a mixer on high until foamy. Gradually add remaining ¼ cup sugar, 1 Tbsp. at a time, until stiff peaks form (tips stand straight). With the mixer running on high, gradually add gelatin mixture to egg white mixture, beating 5 to 7 minutes or until thick (like the consistency of thick, pourable cake batter). Quickly and gently spread marshmallow mixture into prepared pan. Coat another piece of plastic wrap with nonstick coating; place, coated side down, over marshmallow mixture in pan. Chill at least 5 hours or until firm.

5. In a small bowl combine powdered sugar and cornstarch; sprinkle about one-fourth of the mixture evenly onto a large cutting board. Remove plastic wrap from top of marshmallow mixture. Loosen sides of mixture if necessary and carefully invert onto cutting board. Remove plastic wrap or paper. Sprinkle top with some of the remaining powdered sugar mixture. Cut into 1-inch squares. Place squares, about one-third at a time, in a large resealable plastic bag. Add remaining powdered sugar mixture; seal bag and toss to coat all sides of marshmallows with powdered sugar mixture. If desired, use a stencil to dust cocoa powder or gold luster dust over marshmallows.

6. Store marshmallows between sheets of waxed paper or parchment paper in an airtight container in the refrigerator up to 1 week or in the freezer up to 1 month. Makes 80 servings.

*Tip Look for a product that is 100% egg whites.

EGGNOG

Rich eggnog is a hallmark of the Christmas season. For a nonalcoholic version, prepare as directed, except omit the rum and bourbon, and increase the milk to 2⅓ cups.

WHAT YOU NEED

4   egg yolks, beaten
2   cups milk
⅓   cup sugar
1   cup heavy cream
2   Tbsp. light rum (1 oz.)
2   Tbsp. bourbon (1 oz.)
1   tsp. vanilla
    Freshly ground nutmeg

WHAT YOU DO

1. In a large heavy saucepan stir together yolks, milk, and sugar. Cook and stir over medium heat until milk mixture just coats a metal spoon; do not boil. Place pan in a sink or bowl of ice water; stir 2 minutes. Stir in cream, rum, bourbon, and vanilla.
2. Cover and chill 4 to 24 hours. Serve in glasses. Sprinkle with nutmeg. Makes 7 servings.

RASPBERRY HOT CHOCOLATE

Warm up on a cold wintery day with a cup of velvety hot chocolate. For Mexican Hot Chocolate, omit the raspberry syrup, and add 1 teaspoon ground cinnamon and a generous pinch of cayenne pepper with the cream. Serve with long cinnamon sticks.

WHAT YOU NEED

6   cups half-and-half
12 oz. bittersweet or semisweet chocolate, chopped
2   cups heavy cream
½   cup raspberry syrup or raspberry liqueur
1   Tbsp. vanilla
    Sweetened whipped cream (optional)
    Fresh raspberries (optional)
    Chocolate curls (optional)

WHAT YOU DO

1. In a large saucepan or Dutch oven combine half-and-half and chocolate. Cook and stir over medium heat until chocolate is melted and mixture is steaming. Add heavy cream; heat through but do not boil.
2. Whisk well. Stir in raspberry syrup and vanilla. Serve immediately. If desired, top servings with whipped cream, raspberries, and chocolate curls. Makes 12 servings.

Simple Pleasures...
Easy and Elegant

Sit back and relax—you have everything under control with easy yet elegant ideas to make your home a peaceful holiday sanctuary.

VINTAGE CHARM

Sparkling vintage jewelry reflects the spirit of the season when it becomes add-ons to simple candle votives. Set these glittering beauties on a silver tray for a stunningly simple centerpiece.

WHAT YOU NEED

Glass votive candle holders • Paintbrush • Crafts glue • Fine glitter • Vintage jewelry clip earrings • Votive candles • Silver tray

WHAT YOU DO

1. Be sure the glass is clean and dry. Use a paintbrush to paint a thin line of glue around the top of the holder. Dust with glitter. Let dry.

2. Clip the earring or earrings on the edge of the glass holder. Put the candle in the votive. Set the votives on a silver tray.

Never leave a burning candle unattended.

HOLLY JOLLY

Toast your favorite ornaments with a cup of cheer by dressing up a cupboard or buffet with a festooned garland. Made from sturdy twigs painted white, the garland is held strategically in place with clear pushpins. Hang a mix of ornaments in different sizes and colors. Complete the look by tucking in fresh or faux greens and you're ready for the best time of the year.

MAKING SPIRITS BRIGHT

Turn your mantel, shelf, or dining room table into an enchanting Christmas scene. Gather a collection of glass domes in various heights and sizes. Fill a few with vintage ornaments, top each with a saucer plate, then gently turn over and slide into place. Tuck snowy bottle-brush trees under other domes. Wrap up the look with tiny gift packages and mercury glass votives.

BUD BEAUTIES

Gather vintage and mismatched stemware for an eclectic single-stem display. Fill each glass a little over halfway with water, then trim stems to nestle into each vase. We paired carnations, roses, spider mums, and evergreens and eucalyptus sprigs for a festive, colorful combo that gives each a bit of the spotlight.

WINTER WONDERLAND

Let it snow with a glistening, everlasting centerpiece. Cut floral foam to fit a vintage ironstone footbath or casserole dish, then set up a miniature forest of bottle-brush trees. Cover the foam with green sheet moss, top with a mix of pinecones and moss balls, and add a sprinkle of faux snow.

JINGLE ALL THE WAY

Jingle bells in different shapes and sizes fill mismatched goblets to create a last-minute centerpiece that is sure to bring smiles.

WHAT YOU NEED

Mismatched goblets in 3 sizes • Jingle bells in desired colors and sizes • Long serving tray in color to complement colors of bells • Ribbon

WHAT YOU DO

1. Be sure the goblets are clean and dry. Arrange the goblets on the tray from shortest to tallest.
2. Fill the goblets with the jingle bells. Swirl a ribbon at the base of the goblets.

ALL IS BRIGHT

Bring out the magic of the night by dressing up shapely hurricane lanterns with rings of holiday cheer, opposite. Wire favorite greenery and white berries into a garland or tuck in juniper berries or fresh herbs for a fragrant touch. Use thinner fabric-wrapped wire that is easier to bend into the desired shape rather than traditional florists wire.

Never leave a burning candle unattended.

FRESH AND PRETTY

This poinsettia bloom trio has a fun secret ingredient: grapes! For poinsettia best practices, cut stems and place in warm water for 20 minutes to allow the white sap to escape before inserting into grape-filled vase. (This keeps the water from getting cloudy.) Trim and nestle eucalyptus and pittosporum around the mouth of the vase after poinsettias are situated. Check water daily and refill as needed to keep your poinsettia blooms looking fresh.

LOVE AND JOY

Create a merry tabletop with a simple, joyful centerpiece. Lay seeded eucalyptus, pinecones, and Hypericum berries on a plate or charger with a decorative rim. Fill a trio of vintage milk bottles or glass vases with evergreen branches and white and red berry sprigs that will last into the happy new year. Change water daily to keep live greens fresh and fragrant.

GOOD TIDINGS

Spread joy to the world by creating miniature magical moments from a few of your favorite holiday things. Find tree-shape glass funnels at flea markets and science equipment websites. Fill them with glorious ornaments all stacked up for the holidays.

O CHRISTMAS WREATHS

Bring nature inside by gathering petite wreaths made from evergreens and dried herbs. Attach cut greens, berries, and pinecones to wire forms and 3- to 5-inch embroidery hoops using florists wire and hot glue. Leave some embroidery hoops partially exposed for an airy look. Hang wreaths from lengths of ribbon or rickrack at different heights to festively frame your verdant rings.

SILVER BELLS

Dress mint julep cups and silver bowls in red-and-green finery for holiday style. Let them ring-a-ling by filling each one three-fourths full with floral foam, then adding green reindeer moss and sprigs of highbush cranberries or Hypericum berries. Finally, nestle glass votive candle holders inside, making sure each candle stands over the moss and berries. Arrange on a silver tray or platter to celebrate that soon it will be Christmas day.

Never leave a burning candle unattended.

BOWL OF PLENTY

Create a season-long centerpiece that calls on pretty yuletide treasures and requires no watering. Fill a clear glass compote with Christmas ornaments in all shapes and sizes. Mix in a collection of vintage silver napkin rings for merry measure. Set the compote on a white platter adorned with a few more ornaments laid on a bed of seeded eucalyptus. Sprinkle on a little faux snow for a fa, la, la to remember.

SEEING RED

This monochromatic bouquet brings a dose of drama to any tablescape. Cut floral foam to fit desired container then add water. Cut stems at an angle and place a few of the largest blossoms into the foam to gauge the general scale and shape of the arrangement. Add greenery and more large flowers, followed by smaller flowers to fill in gaps and lend visual interest. Glue red ornaments to the ends of plant stakes and tuck them among the stems. Remove leaves from any part of the stem that will be submerged in water to help water stay fresh longer.

Citrus and Spice

Experience comfort and joy with motifs and aromas that make a country Christmas the one you'll always remember.

CITRUS AND SPICE TREE

Make your holiday just a little bit cozier with fresh ornaments you make yourself. Pot a fresh evergreen in a simple container and then fill the tree with dried orange slices, tiny chalkboard greetings, and old-fashioned gingerbread trims. Make extra ornaments to use as clever package toppers.

FESTIVE PACKAGE TOPPERS

A simple gingerbread cookie or tiny chalkboard greeting can become the focal point of a special package. Make a hole in the cookie before baking using a plastic straw. Thread a piece of bakers twine through the hole to attach.

GINGERBREAD COOKIE TREE TOPPER

Aromatic orange slices and a happy gingerbread cookie stand up straight to make your tree complete. To make the quick and clever topper for your citrus and spice tree, use hot glue to glue three dried orange slices together with a gingerbread man in the middle. Glue the arrangement to a wooden skewer and wire to the top of the tree

TINY CHALKBOARD MESSAGES

Live-edge wood discs become expressions of the season when they are painted and decorated for the tree.

WHAT YOU NEED

Wood discs, available at crafts stores • Sandpaper • Drill and ⅛-inch drill bit • Black chalkboard paint • Paintbrush • White chalkboard pen • Twine

WHAT YOU DO

1. Sand the wood discs to be sure they are smooth. Drill a hole at the top for hanging.
2. Paint a circle in the middle of the disc using the chalkboard paint. Let dry.
3. Write a message on the painted disc using the chalkboard pen.
4. Thread twine through the hole for hanging.

NATURALLY CITRUS ORNAMENTS

Orange slices are dried and then strung with twine for a
simply aromatic trim.

WHAT YOU NEED

Fresh oranges • Sharp knife • Paper towels • Hydrogen
peroxide • Salt • Sheet pan • Parchment paper • Twine

WHAT YOU DO

1. Wash and dry the oranges. Slice the oranges about
⅜-inch thick and lay on a paper towel. Drizzle each orange
with hydrogen peroxide and sprinkle with salt. Blot using
paper towels to dry as much as possible.

2. Preheat oven to 225°F. Place parchment paper on a sheet
pan and arrange oranges about 1 inch apart on the pan.
Put pan in oven for 2 to 3 hours, turning the oranges at least
twice. When the oranges seem dried, remove from oven and
cool. Thread twine through the tops for hanging.

Do not eat, for decoration only.

COUNTRY SPICE POMANDERS

Oranges and whole spices combine with snippets of evergreen and pinecones to make a stunning centerpiece for your holiday table.

WHAT YOU NEED

Fresh oranges • Pencil • Toothpicks or skewers • Whole cloves • Anise stars • Hot-glue gun and glue sticks • Evergreen sprigs • Cinnamon sticks • Pinecones • Fresh cranberries

WHAT YOU DO

1. Wash and dry the oranges. Use a pencil to mark the design where you want it on the oranges. Use a toothpick to make holes where the design is marked. Place a whole clove in each hole. If the anise star has a stem, place it in a poked hole. If not, use a dot of hot glue to secure.

2. Arrange the evergreen sprigs, cinnamon sticks, and pinecones in a low container.

3. Arrange the oranges on top. Sprinkle fresh cranberries over the arrangement.

COZY BUTTON & YARN BALLS

Foam balls are wrapped with textured yarn and topped with vintage buttons to make cozy ornaments for your tree or to display in a vintage enamelware bowl.

WHAT YOU NEED

3-inch foam balls such as Styrofoam • Yarn in desired colors and textures • Straight pins • Scissors • Hot-glue gun and glue sticks • Buttons • Bakers twine

WHAT YOU DO

1. Plan the design you want to make. Starting at one end of the ball, pin one end of the yarn in place. Wrap the yarn around the ball using hot glue if necessary to secure. Completely wrap the ball with the yarn, using hot glue to tack the yarn at the end.

2. Thread bakers twine through the holes of a button and tie a knot or bow. Glue the button to the top of the ornament.

FARMHOUSE VELVETEEN STOCKING

Velveteen and ticking combine to create a touch of farmhouse nostalgia and a perfect place for Santa to hide his goodies.

WHAT YOU NEED

¼ yard seersucker fabric • ¼ yard velveteen fabric • Scissors • Sewing thread to match fabrics • Small piece of eucalyptus • Small clothespin

WHAT YOU DO

1. Enlarge and trace templates, opposite, and cut out. Use the stocking template to cut a front and a back, reversing one of the shapes. Repeat for the lining. With right sides together, stitch cuff on two short and one long side. Clip corners, turn, and press.

2. Stitch stocking pieces with right sides together, leaving top edge open and using a ½-inch seam. Clip curves. Turn right side out.

3. Stitch lining pieces with right sides together, using ½-inch seam. Trim the seam close to stitching. Insert lining inside turned stocking, keeping top straight edge even. Pin right side of cuff to inside lining of stocking and stitch, leaving cuff ends open. Turn cuff to outside of stocking and press.

4. Use a clothespin to clip a piece of eucalyptus to the cuff of the stocking.

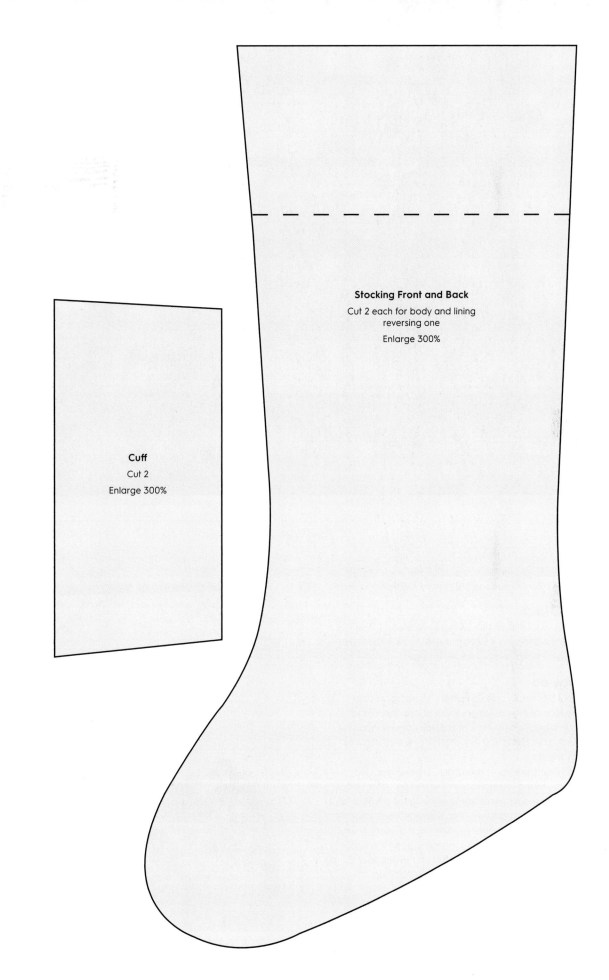

Cuff
Cut 2
Enlarge 300%

Stocking Front and Back
Cut 2 each for body and lining
reversing one
Enlarge 300%

BIRDIE ICE TREATS

Glistening in the sun, these ice sculptures are pretty to look at and a Christmas treat for your feathered friends.

WHAT YOU NEED

Wax carton milk containers • Scissors • Water • Twine • Clothespin • Birdseed • Pieces of evergreen • Cranberries • Orange slices and rinds • Freezer • Skewer

WHAT YOU DO

1. Rinse out the empty milk containers. Use scissors to cut down the tops of the containers to be about 5 inches tall. Fill the containers with water. Cut a piece of twine about 8 inches long and loop into the water. Use a clothespin to secure to the sides.

2. Add birdseed, pieces of evergreen, cranberries, and orange slices to the water. Place in the freezer. After about 1 hour, check the containers. Some of the items will float, so poke them down with a skewer into the semi-frozen water. Readjust the twine if necessary. Do this about every hour if you want the items to be distributed throughout the water. Freeze until firm. Remove from freezer and take paper off of the frozen block. Hang in a tree or on plant holders.

WINTERTIME MESSAGES

You can make chalkboards to express yourself using black or clear chalkboard paint. Below, a slab of wood was sanded and then painted with charcoal chalkboard paint before the holiday phrases were added. If you want to keep the wood surface natural, paint the wood stump or slab with clear chalkboard paint. First, sand the stump or chunk of wood. Then paint three coats of clear chalkboard paint on the surface, waiting for each coat to dry before painting the next one. Then grab some chalk and wish the entire outdoors a Merry Christmas!

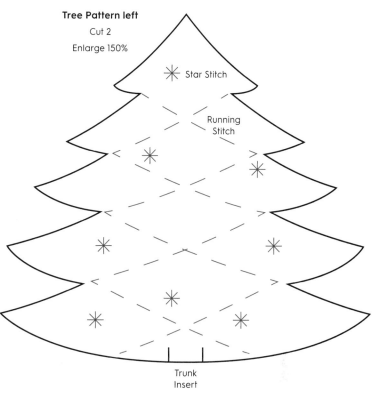

Tree Pattern left
Cut 2
Enlarge 150%

Star Stitch

Running
Stitch

Trunk
Insert

BEAUTIFULLY EMBROIDERED TREES

Create your own one-of-a-kind embroidered felt tree to hang on your evergreen or to embellish your front doorknob. A tiny stick serves as a trunk in this mini evergreen beauty.

WHAT YOU NEED
Nonwoven felt such as National Nonwovens in desired shades of dark green • Embroidery floss in desired colors • Embroidery needle • Scissors • Polyester fiberfill • Small stick • Crafts glue

WHAT YOU DO
1. Copy and trace the templates, right. Trace around the templates on the green felt, cutting two pieces for each tree.
2. Referring to the embroidery stitches on the pattern and in the photo, embroider onto the front piece of each tree. Lay the front on the back piece and use small whipstitches to sew the two pieces together, leaving a hole in the bottom for stuffing and for trunk placement. Stuff the trees with fiberfill and glue the stick in the bottom for a trunk. Let dry. Thread a piece of embroidery floss through the top for a hanger. (See page 158 for Stitch Diagrams.)

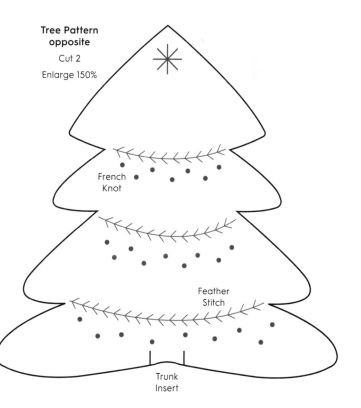

Tree Pattern opposite
Cut 2
Enlarge 150%

French
Knot

Feather
Stitch

Trunk
Insert

WINTER BERRY BANNER

This elegant country banner will welcome your guests for the holidays with its intricate appliqué and embroidery. The heirloom-quality piece is perfect for an all-season winter banner.

FINISHED SIZE
12×14 inches

WHAT YOU NEED

FOR THE BACKGROUND
14×26-inch rectangle white or cream wool

FOR THE APPLIQUÉ
Two 6×8-inch rectangles in different shades (light and medium) of textured cream wool for leaves and stems • 8×12-inch rectangle textured taupe wool (dark) for leaves and stems • Four 6-inch squares in different shades (light to dark) orange wool for berries

FOR THE FREEZER PAPER
18-inch square

FOR THE FUSIBLE WEFT OR FUSIBLE INTERFACING
14×26-inch rectangle

FOR THE PAPER-BACKED FUSIBLE WEB
17×30-inch rectangle

FOR THE BACKING FABRIC
15×27-inch rectangle cream cotton

FOR THE STITCHING
Cream, taupe, and orange variegated size No. 12 pearl cotton or embroidery floss (Shown: Valdani size No. 12 pearl cotton, colors #12, #178 and #244) (See page 158 for Stitch Diagrams.)

WHAT YOU DO

PREPARING BACKGROUND AND APPLIQUÉ PIECES
1. Fuse the weft or interfacing to the wrong side of the background.
2. Using the Winter Berry Banner Patterns on page 72, trace the number of pieces indicated on each pattern on the dull side of the freezer paper.
3. Fuse a 2½×12-inch rectangle of paper-backed fusible web at one end of the back of the taupe wool. Cut six ³⁄₁₆×12-inch-long stems and two ¼×4-inch-long stems.
4. Fuse a 1×4-inch rectangle of paper-backed fusible web at one end of the back of each of the cream wools. Cut three ¼×4-inch-long stems from each.
5. Iron the freezer paper leaf, ribbon, and berry patterns to the right side of appropriate wools. Iron Berry A patterns to the darkest orange, then iron Berries B, C and D to progressively lighter orange wools.
6. Cut out around each pattern on the traced lines.

STITCHING THE APPLIQUÉ
1. Referring to Layout Diagram, hand stitch a thread X to mark the five corners of the background.
2. Referring to the diagram, remove the paper, arrange and pin the leaves and corresponding 4-inch-long stems

to the background keeping all at least ½ inch from the future edges.
3. Using a Blanket Stitch, stitch the leaves with the corresponding cream or taupe pearl cotton. Using a backstitch, stitch down the middle of the stems.
4. Remove the paper backing, arrange and pin the 12-inch-long stems positioning breaks in the stems where berries will cover them. Using taupe pearl cotton, couch using a diagonal stitch over the stems.
5. Remove the paper, arrange and pin the berries on the stems. Using orange pearl cotton stitch French Knots in the middle of each berry, using 3, 4, 5, and 6 knots as the berries get larger. Arrange the two ribbon pieces and backstitch with orange pearl cotton.

FINISHING THE PROJECT
1. Fuse a 15×25-inch piece of paper-backed fusible web to the wrong side of the backing fabric. Remove paper and fuse to the back of the stitched banner, pressing from the middle to the sides and ends.
2. Trim the fused project to diagram measurements, using the stitched X's as a guide.
3. Using cream pearl cotton, blanket stitch around the edges.
4. Cut two 1½×3½-inch rectangles from corner trimmings. Blanket stitch around the edges. Fold each over to form a loop and stitch bottom together. Position on the back of the top edge about 1½ inches in from each corner. Stitch in place. Place a rod or sanded stick in the loops for hanging.
Tip: When working with white wool, be sure all of your work surfaces are clean. If shedding from orange berries gets on the background, carefully remove with lint roller or tape.

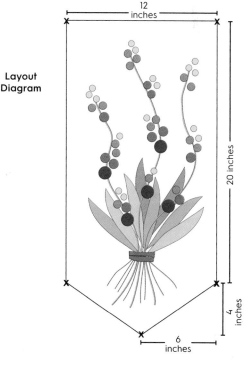

Layout Diagram

12 inches

20 inches

4 inches

6 inches

Winter Berry Banner Patterns

Leaf A

Trace 4
Cut: 1 dark, 2 medium, 1 light

Leaf B

Trace 4
Cut: 1 dark, 1 medium, 2 light

Ribbon

Cut 1
Cut apart on dashed line.

Berry A

Cut 5

Berry B

Cut 8

Berry C

Cut 18

Berry D

Cut 17

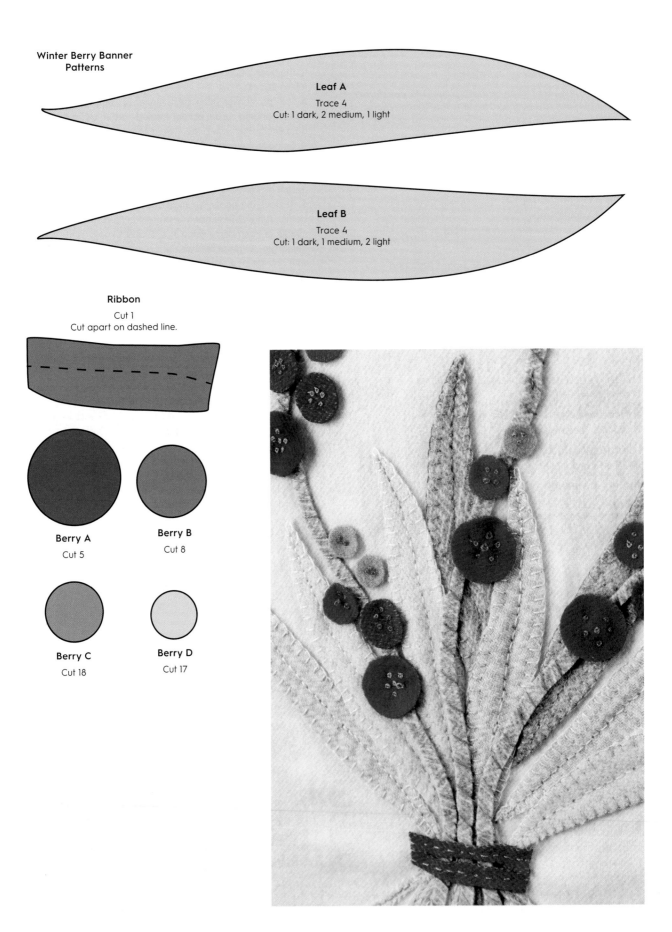

FALL INTO WINTER WREATH

With the rose gold tone of this stunning wreath, it can be enjoyed for months before and after Christmas as well as during the holidays. Touches of sparkling metallic paints highlight the nature finds.

WHAT YOU NEED

Grapevine wreath form • White spray paint • Foam brush• Pinecones • White craft paint • Acorns • Feathers • Faux foliage • Hot-glue gun and glue sticks • Rose gold spray paint • Gold spray paint • Wide orange ribbon

WHAT YOU DO

1. Lay the wreath form on a flat surface and plan the design. Spray the wreath form with white spray paint. Let dry.
2. Use a foam brush to paint the tips of the pinecones with white crafts paint. Let dry.
3. Use the rose gold and gold spray paint to paint the acorns and faux foliage. Let dry.
4. Arrange the elements on the wreath and adhere with hot glue. Let dry. Loop the ribbon around the top for hanging.

MARVELOUS MOSS

Spanish moss, feathery mood moss, and lime green reindeer moss cover a straw wreath form to create a lush, carpet-like base for an assortment of pinecones.

WHAT YOU NEED

Bags of moss in various colors such as Spanish moss, feathery mood moss and lime green reindeer moss • Paper towels • Straw wreath • Pinecones • Hot-glue gun and glue sticks • Light pink pepperberries

WHAT YOU DO

1. Bags of moss sold at crafts supply stores are often dried out and clumped together. Lay moss on a paper towel and spritz with water to make it more pliable and easier to work with.
2. Lay the straw wreath on a flat surface. Hot glue the moss to the wreath. Hot glue the pinecones facing different directions, snuggling some in point first, until the wreath feels full but still allows the moss to show.
3. Tuck and glue small bunches of light pink pepperberries among the pinecones to enhance the romantic appeal.

CINNAMON AND CITRUS WREATH

A simple grapevine wreath is the base for this unconventional display. Begin with a layer of juniper, cedar sprigs, and magnolia leaves. Next, generously pile on dried citrus slices (see page 62 for how to make them), overlapping and hot-gluing in place as you go. Silver brunia berries and seeded eucalyptus act as tiny ornaments, peeking above and below the translucent slices. Tie and secure bundles of cinnamon sticks with twine for the final aromatic touch.

FARMHOUSE CHRISTMAS CRACKERS

The most widely accepted story about the famous Christmas cracker or popper is that they were invented in the mid-1840s by a London pastry cook by wrapping sugared almonds and other sweets in a twist of colored paper. A more common version today is making the crackers using cardboard tubes covered with paper. The sweet surprise or candy is hidden inside and the cracker must be broken in two pieces to find the candy. We used brown kraft paper and simple stamps to make these old-fashioned, full-of-fun table favors.

WHAT YOU NEED
Brown kraft paper • Scissors • Rubber stamp • Black ink stamp pad • Paper towel rolls • Candy • Transparent tape • Black-and-white bakers twine

WHAT YOU DO
1. Cut the kraft paper into 10×12-inch pieces. Use the rubber stamp and ink pad to print a design on the paper. Set aside to dry.
2. Cut the paper towel roll to 6 inches. Cut that length in half.
3. Lay the printed paper on a flat surface and lay the cut paper towel roll on the paper. Fill each side with candy or surprises. Put the two halves back together and tape to hold. Wrap the paper around the cardboard and twist the ends. Tie pieces of bakers twine around each end and tie a knot and bow to secure.
4. To open, break or crack the cracker in half to reveal the candy or surprise.

Soft and Sweet

Celebrate the spirit of the season with handmade crafts and decorations that are simply soft, stunning, and sweet.

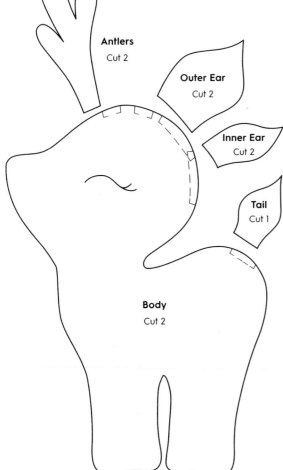

Antlers
Cut 2

Outer Ear
Cut 2

Inner Ear
Cut 2

Tail
Cut 1

Body
Cut 2

REINDEER GAMES

These snowy little darlings almost bounce with the joy of the season. The baby reindeer with their pink ears and tails add delight to a stocking, tree, or gift.

WHAT YOU NEED

Nonwoven felt such as National Nonwoven in soft hues, brown, and dark pink • Disappearing-ink marking pen • Scissors • Brown embroidery floss • Embroidery needle • Fabric glue • Straight pins • 6-inch length of white string (optional) • Polyester fiberfill • Small pink pom-pom

WHAT YOU DO

1. Trace patterns, left, onto white paper; cut out. Using a disappearing-ink marking pen, trace each shape onto appropriate felt color the number of times indicated on the patterns; cut out.
2. Use two strands of embroidery floss for all embroidery. Using brown embroidery floss, stitch the eye with a few curving backstitches and the eyelashes with two small Straight Stitches. (See page 158 for Stitch Diagrams.)
3. Glue pink inner ear pieces to white ear pieces. Pin together reindeer front and back pieces with wrong sides together. Insert the antlers, ears, and tail between the layers. If desired, enclose string ends between layers for a hanging loop. Using white floss, whipstitch around the body; stuff reindeer with polyester fiberfill as you stitch, leaving an opening along the chest. Stuff reindeer firmly through opening. Stitch opening closed. Glue tiny pom-pom onto snout.

PASTEL CROCHET WREATHS

Simple to make and beautiful to display, these little crochet wreaths are made using the chain stitch and then attached to a simple metal hoop. Make them in all shades of green for your holiday decorating.

WHAT YOU NEED

Medium-weight yarn in desired colors and style
● #H Crochet hook ● 4-inch metal ring ● Needle

WHAT YOU DO

Remove the desired amount of yarn from the skein for each wreath.

CROCHET

ROW 1: Tie a slip knot onto the crochet hook. Chain stitch to the desired length, enough to go around the perimeter of the metal ring.

ROW 2: In each chain, crochet a single stitch. Continue until the end of the string. Fasten off the end.

Thread a needle with yarn. Attach crocheted piece to the hoop by slip stitching the top of the first crocheted strand to the bottom of the other crocheted strand. When you've reached the end, knot and trim edges. Hang with ribbon or yarn.

SWEET CROCHET-WRAPPED TREES

The crochet yarn creates the texture on these gentle trees.

WHAT YOU NEED

Cardboard tree form, available at crafts stores • Yarn in desired color • #H Crochet hook • Hot-glue gun and glue sticks • 12-inch piece of velveteen ribbon • Scissors

WHAT YOU DO

To determine the length of the finished string, hold the yarn at the bottom of the tree form and wrap the yarn around, every ¼ inch until you've reached the top. Release the yarn and measure the length.

CROCHET:

ROW 1: Tie a slip knot onto the crochet hook. Chain-stitch to desired length (measured in previous step).

ROW 2: In the first chain, crochet one half double stitch. In the second chain, crochet two double stitches. In the third chain, crochet one half double stitch. In the fourth chain, crochet one slip stitch. Continue this pattern until the end of the string is completed. Fasten off the end.

Using hot-glue, attach the string to cardboard form, starting at the base and wrapping around, overlapping by ¼ to ½ inch. Continue until the top. Trim/hide any extra strands of yarn. Tie a bow with the velveteen ribbon and glue to the top of the tree. Trim the ends.

DOGGY DONUT

Whether your little best friend is a rescue pup or a playful pedigree, he will love this doggy toy you made just for him.

WHAT YOU NEED

9×12-inch pieces of terry cloth in desired pattern and color
• Piping in desired color • Sewing thread to match fabric
• Polyester fiberfill

WHAT YOU DO

1. Enlarge and trace the pattern, right. Cut out two pieces. Stay stitch inner circle ¼ inch from the edge on both pieces. Clip curves.

2. Baste edges of inner circle ¼ inch while turning under to wrong side.

3. Baste piping around outer edge of top circle. Place top and bottom circle right sides together and stitch together on outside edge, being sure to catch piping in stitching.

4. Turn donut shape right side out. Hand stitch inner circles together leaving a small opening for adding stuffing.

5. Stuff firmly. Hand-stitch small opening closed.

Donut

Cut 2
Enlarge 150%

VERY MERRY GNOMES

A simple felt shape wraps up to make a gnome hat that tops a handmade pom-pom. Add a hat topper and nose and you have a soft and sweet holiday trim.

WHAT YOU NEED

2×3-inch piece of cardboard • White cotton yarn • 12-inch piece of yarn • Scissors • Nonwoven felt such as National Nonwovens in desired colors • 12-inch piece of coordinating ribbon • Hot-glue gun and glue sticks • Small wool balls, available at crafts stores • Narrow ribbon

WHAT YOU DO

1. To make the pom-pom, wrap the yarn around the cardboard piece about 100 times keeping the yarn as even as possible. Carefully remove from cardboard and slide the 12-inch piece of yarn through the loop. Tie with a double knot. Cut through all the loops of yarn at the other end. Shake the pom-pom and trim. Set aside. See illustration, below, for making pom-poms of all sizes.
2. To make the hat, trace the pattern, below, and cut out. Place on desired color of felt and cut out. Wrap the felt around to make a cone, overlapping as indicated on the pattern. Secure with hot glue. Place the pom-pom inside the hat and secure with hot glue. Glue the ribbon around the bottom of the hat. Glue the wool balls to the top of hat and on the pom-pom for a nose. Sew a ribbon to top to hang.

HOW TO MAKE A POM-POM

1. Wrap yarn many times around a piece of cardboard, fork, book, or other object depending on the size of pom-pom desired (A).
2. Tie the entire bundle in the center and slide the yarn from the object (B).
3. Cut the looped yarn at both ends of the bundle (C).
4. Trim yarn ends to desired length (D) and fluff the yarn.

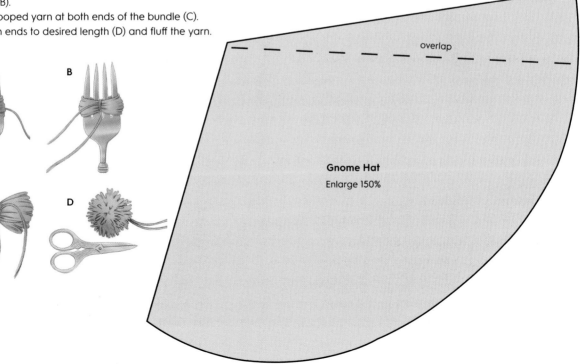

Gnome Hat
Enlarge 150%

overlap

SOFTY ST. NICK

This jolly old elf is sure to become a favorite friend during the holidays with his happy smile and soft, white beard.

WHAT YOU NEED

Sport-weight/Fine (2) or DK-weight/Light (3) acrylic/wool blend yarn: white, pink, red • Knitting needles: US 1.5 (2.5-millimeter) • Needles: yarn and sewing • Polyester fiberfill • Sewing thread: white, black, red • 25-millimeter round button (nose) • 2 round 16- to 18-millimeter shank buttons: black • 10—19-millimeter buttons • ½ yard of white cotton fabric

WHAT YOU DO

FINISHED PILLOW SIZE: 15½×17½ INCHES

Gauge: 29 sts × 40 rows = 4 inches
Take time to check your gauge.
Note: See Knitting Abbreviations, page 158.

KNIT THE PILLOW

With white yarn, cast on 106 sts.
Rows 1–4: Knit.
Rows 5–16: Work St st starting with a knit row.
Row 17: K105, kfb (107 sts).
Row 18: P106, pfb (108 sts).
Rows 19–72: Work St st starting with a knit row. Change to pink yarn.
Rows 73–110: Work St st starting with a knit row. Change to white yarn.
Rows 111–124: Knit. Change to red yarn.
Rows 125–350: Work St st starting with a knit row.
Rows 351–354: Knit. Make the buttonholes in the next row.
Row 355: K8, *cast off 2 sts without knitting them, cast on 2 sts using backwards loop cast-on method, K8.* Rep from * to * 9 times to make 10 buttonholes.
Rows 356–359: Knit.
Cast off. Cut yarn, leaving a long tail. Block the pillow piece so it lies flat.

KNIT AND ADD THE MUSTACHE

Cast on 10 sts with white.
Rows 1–2: Knit.
Row 3: K9, kfb (11 sts).
Row 4: K10, kfb (12 sts).
Row 5: K11, kfb (13 sts).
Row 6: K12, kfb (14 sts).
Row 7: K13, kfb (15 sts).
Row 8: K14, kfb (16 sts).
Row 9: K15, kfb (17 sts).
Row 10: K16, kfb (18 sts).
Row 11: K17, kfb (19 sts).
Row 12: K18, kfb (20 sts).
Row 13: K19, kfb (21 sts).
Row 14: K20, kfb (22 sts).
Row 15: K21, kfb (23 sts).
Row 16: K22, kfb (24 sts).
Rows 17–18: Knit.

Row 19: K22, k2tog (23 sts).
Row 20: K21, k2tog (22 sts).
Row 21: K20, k2tog (21 sts).
Row 22: K19, k2tog (20 sts).
Row 23: K18, k2tog (19 sts).
Row 24: K17, k2tog (18 sts).
Row 25: K16, k2tog (17 sts).
Row 26: K15, k2tog (16 sts).
Row 27: K14, k2tog (15 sts).
Row 28: K13, k2tog (14 sts).
Row 29: K12, k2tog (13 sts).
Row 30: K11, k2tog (12 sts).
Row 31: K10, k2tog (11 sts).
Row 32: K9, k2tog (10 sts).
Row 33: K8, k2tog (9 sts).
Row 34: K7, k2tog (8 sts).
Row 35: K6, k2tog (7 sts).
Row 36: K5, k2tog (6 sts).

1. Cut yarn, leaving a long tail. Thread tail through sts on the yarn needle and draw up tightly. Whipstitch row edges together, leaving an opening for stuffing. Stuff slightly with fiberfill; stitch opening closed.
2. Repeat to make a second mustache piece.
3. Referring to photo, use sewing needle and white thread to sew bottoms of corners of mustache pieces to pillow cover.

KNIT AND ADD THE NOSE

1. Cast on 13 sts with red yarn. Work 15 rows of St st. Cast off. Cut yarn, leaving a long tail.
2. Using sewing needle and red thread, stitch a circle of running sts around the edge of the knitted piece, leaving a tail. Place 25-millimeter button in center. Pull tail to cinch knitted piece around button; tie off. Use yarn needle and red yarn to stitch nose over mustache. Straight-stitch a mouth.

KNIT AND ADD THE EYEBROWS

Cast on 13 sts with white yarn.
Rows 1–2: Knit.
Row 3: K1, *k2tog, K1.* Rep from * to * 3 times (9 sts).
Rows 4–5: Knit.
Cast off. Cut yarn, leaving a long tail.
Repeat to make a second eyebrow.
Referring to photo, use sewing needle and black thread to stitch 16- to 18-millimeter buttons to pillow front for eyes. Use yarn needle and white yarn to stitch eyebrows above eyes.

FINISHING

1. Match the cast-off edge with the row of increases (Rows 17–18). Mattress-stitch side seams using matching yarn and yarn needle. Do not secure the button flap.
2. Sew buttons onto button flap, aligning each button with a buttonhole.
3. Measure finished pillow cover. Cut two cotton fabric pieces to measured size plus ⅜-inch seam allowances for a pillow form. With right sides together and leaving a 4-inch opening along one edge, sew together. Stuff with polyester fiberfill and hand-sew opening closed. Insert pillow form into knitted pillow cover and fasten buttons.

GRINCH-PROOF STOCKINGS

With their cotton-candy colors and quirky shapes, these delightful stockings look like they could hang from fireplaces in Whoville. Gather colorful felt and embroidery floss, plus a sprinkling of beads, to whip up a creative assortment of these holiday stockings.

WHAT YOU NEED

5×8-inch piece of non-woven felt such as National Nonwovens, in light blue, dark pink, yellow-green, or blue-green • Assorted scraps of felt in teal, red, light pink, dark pink, aqua, and/or blue • Embroidery floss in colors to match felt • Straight pins • Embroidery and sewing needles • Assorted pearl bead • Polyester fiberfill • 12-inch length of ⅛-inch-wide ribbon

WHAT YOU DO

1. Trace patterns, opposite, onto white paper; cut out. Trace each shape onto appropriate felt color. Cut out shapes on traced lines. (See page 158 for Stitch Diagrams.)

2. Referring to the photo, above, and dashed placement lines on stocking patterns, pin heel, toe, and/or cuff pieces to stocking front. Using an embroidery needle and two strands of matching embroidery floss, whipstitch the inside edges of each piece to stocking front.

Note: The outside edges will be stitched when the front and back stockings are stitched together.

3. Referring to photo and stocking patterns, pin stripes, circles, diamonds, or teardrops to stocking front. Whipstitch the pieces to the stocking. Stitch beads to the stripes, circles, diamonds, or teardrops.

4. Pin the stocking front to stocking back. Whipstitch shapes together, using matching embroidery floss and leaving a 1½-inch opening along the side opposite toe.

Note: When stitching the toe of stocking A, push a small amount of fiberfill into the end of the toe.

5. Using the eraser end of a pencil, push fiberfill into the stocking through the opening. Whipstitch opening closed.

6. Using matching embroidery floss, stitch the center of the ribbon to cuff corner. Tie the ribbon into a bow.

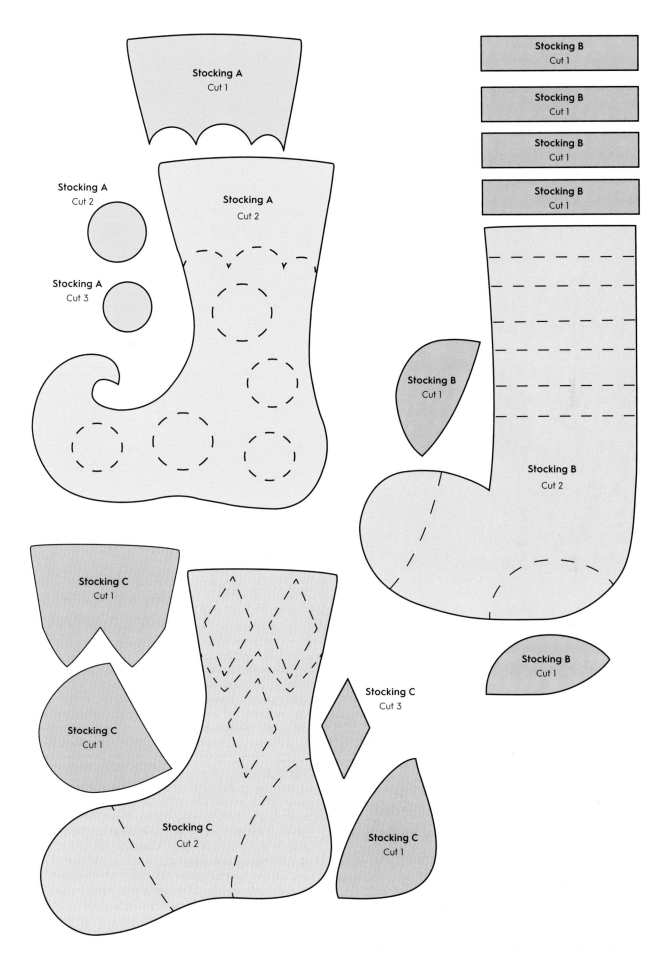

HOLLY-TOPPED TRIMS

These elegant trims combine the classic Christmas holly-leaf shape, a bit of elegant embroidery, and some happy jingle-bell berries.

Each ornament shown has five or six leaves and six red bells.

WHAT YOU NEED
Nonwoven felt such as National Nonwovens in light, medium, and dark teal green • Freezer paper • Light teal green No. 24 pearl silk or No. 12 pearl cotton • Three ¼-inch red jingle bells • 3- or 4-inch-diameter white ball ornament • Crafts glue

WHAT YOU DO
1. Using templates, above, trace the number of pieces desired on the dull side of the freezer paper. For each leaf trace one A/B set or one C/D set. Make 5 or 6 leaves.
2. Using different color values for each A and B in a set or C and D in a set, iron the freezer paper leaf patterns to one side of appropriate felt. Cut out around each pattern on the traced line.
3. Remove the papers and arrange a B leaf on top of each A leaf and a D leaf on top of each C leaf. Using a Feather Stitch and the silk or cotton thread, stitch a center vein through each layered leaf. (See page 158 for Stitch Diagrams.)
4. Referring to the photograph, group two or three embellished leaves together and stitch on two or three bells. Arrange groups of holly on each ornament and secure in place with crafts glue.

Nose

COZY SWEATER SNOWMAN

You'll fall in love with this soft and sweet little fellow.

WHAT YOU NEED
Recycled cream-color or white sweater • Scissors • Foam balls such as Styrofoam in two sizes • Hot-glue gun and glue sticks • String • Ribbon • Orange yarn pom-pom • Black beads • Orange felt • Wool balls

WHAT YOU DO
1. Lay the sweater on a flat surface. Cut a sleeve off of the sweater. Set aside.

2. Using a knife, shave a bit off the top and bottom of foam balls so they stack nicely. Place both balls inside the sweater sleeve. Fold and secure the sweater on the underside of the snowman with hot glue.

3. Tie a string around the neck to bunch the fabric. Top with a bow tied around the neck. At the top of the snowman, tie a string around the fabric and fold over the top of the sleeve. Adhere the orange yarn pom-pom to the top of the hat.

4. For the nose, roll the orange felt into a cone using the template, above, as a guide. Attach with hot glue.

5. Glue black beads onto face for eyes and mouth. Cut wool balls in half and glue for buttons.

Wrap Up the Cheer...
for Christmas Day!

You'll be wrapped and ready when you dress up those precious gifts with clever gift wraps and handmade greeting cards that are sure to bring a smile!

SPELLED-OUT GREETINGS

Letter tiles from a word tile game send merry messages when they become part of your holiday wrap. First wrap the gift with your favorite paper and add a wide strip of scrapbook paper. Then spell out your happy message by attaching the little tile messages with a hot-glue gun. Add a bow and you are ready to go.

MR. SNOWMAN WRAP AND CARD

For a special gift wrap, make a happy holiday snowman to adorn a wrapped package. Then make a simple tag and greeting card to match.

WHAT YOU NEED

Small piece of orange clay such as Playdoh • Gift wrapped in blue paper • Foam balls, such as Styrofoam, in three sizes • Knife • Decoupage medium • Foam brush • Chunky white glitter • Glue stick • 7 small black beads • Ribbon

WHAT YOU DO

1. Make a tiny cone shape from the orange clay. Set aside to dry. Cut each of the foam balls in half using a knife and arrange from biggest (bottom) to smallest (top). Where the balls meet, trim a bit from the top/bottom.

2. Using a foam brush, coat the balls with decoupage medium and cover with chunky white glitter. Let dry. When dry, attach to wrapped present using hot glue. Attach the clay nose, bead eyes and mouth, and a ribbon with hot glue.

FOR THE GIFT TAG

Glue three half-circle beads onto a gift tag. Use a permanent marker to add eyes. Punch a hole in the tag and tie at snowman's neck.

FOR THE GREETING CARD

Cut a snowflake from blue paper. Adhere to front of a blank card. Dust with glitter. Stamp a Christmas message at the top.

PUTTING ON THE RITZ

Make any package ultra festive with unexpected baubles, glitzy ribbons, and handcrafted trims. Decked in coral and red party-store pom-poms and confetti-ish sequins, a sprightly present puts a fresh face on seasonal style. Starting with a white backdrop lets you add fun forms in varying hues.

MERRY MEDALLION

Resembling a major award, a drink coaster, left, sports a merry motif and glittery ribbon tails and provides a prize-worthy profile atop a gift wrapped with simple white paper and gold-edged ribbon.

SEASONAL GREENS

Organic references (linen paper, a berry pick, and cotton ribbon) complement a stamped-in-place holly sprig, below. Create a harmonizing gift tag by stamping on a message that expresses seasonal wishes.

COOKIE CUTTER FUN

*Rows of white flakes on bright red paper are suitable
topped with snowflake cookie cutters in two sizes. The
cutest ribbon with tiny snowball edging completes the
totally cool package.*

*For a simpler version using cookie cutters, choose a
vintage red plastic cutter and tie it to a white package
with striped ribbon. So easy...so fun!*

CHRISTMAS WISHES
SNOWFLAKE CARD

Rubber stamping and confetti stickers make this sweet card so easy to create. Be sure to add a lovely message inside the card for each and every one on your holiday list.

WHAT YOU NEED

5×8-inch piece of blue cardstock • 4½×7½-inch piece of white paper • Glue stick • Snowflake rubber stamp • Message rubber stamp • Blue stamp pad • Fine white glitter • Adhesive-back confetti snowflakes

WHAT YOU DO

1. Score the blue cardstock in half and fold to make a card. Repeat with the white paper. Place the white paper over the blue paper and glue with glue stick. Open the card.

2. Use the snowflake stamp to make images on the front of the card. Use the message stamp to make the greeting. Dust with white glitter while still damp. Adhere the confetti snowflakes to the front of the card.

3. For the inside of the card, print off the verse in desired font. Cut out and glue inside the card. Use your finger and crafts glue to make light fingerprints on the card; dust with glitter. Let dry. Add confetti to inside of card if desired.

INSIDE VERSE:

Snowflakes floating down
to greet you with gentle kisses
May snow tuck you in
and quiet the world

Holly and ivy, silver and gold,
hot drinks are waiting,
to warm up your soul.

Cheers to Christmas
And a Happy New Year

RED BIRD GREETING CARD

Pretty scrapbook papers and a sweet message are all it takes to create a must-keep greeting card for your family and friends.

WHAT YOU NEED

12×6-inch piece of patterned cardstock • 5½×5½-inch piece of white paper • Gold pen • Red cardstock • Light green paper • Paper punch • Black permanent pen • Glue stick

WHAT YOU DO

1. Score the patterned cardstock in half and fold to make a square card shape. Glue the white paper in the center of the card front using a glue stick. Use the gold pen to make a 5-inch circle on the front of the card. **TIP:** Use a bowl, small plate, or other round object to draw around for ease in making the circle. Set aside.

2. Trace the template, above. Cut out. Cut the pieces for the bird and leaves. Use a paper punch to make berries from the red paper.

3. Use a glue stick to glue the pieces in place, referring to the photo and pattern for placement. Use the fine black pen to make the legs and eyes.

4. For the inside of the card, print off the verse in desired font. Cut out and glue inside the card.

INSIDE VERSE:

> Holly and ivy, silver and gold,
> hot drinks are waiting,
> to warm up your soul.
>
> Cheers to Christmas
> And a Happy New Year

ONE-STAMP WONDERS

The smallest rubber stamps can produce big results. Use them for tiny packages or clever gift tags. Repeat an image in a circle to fashion a wreath, or stamp in multiple rows to form an overall pattern. Repeat evergreen branches all over for a bushy corner effect or stamp over each other for a pretty pattern.

KEEP-YOUR-MARBLES CARDS

This project is so fun and unpredictable, it is sure to become a family card-making tradition. Marbles are put in a box with paint and a piece of cardstock, and the unexpected colors and patterns are always a fun surprise!

WHAT YOU NEED

Shoebox or other toss-away box • Masking tape • Marbles • Blank cardstock card • Acrylic paint in desired colors • Stickers

WHAT YOU DO

1. Set the shoebox on a flat surface. Cut a piece of masking tape and put in one area of the card front to keep a blank space.

2. Put the marbles and cardstock card into the box. Squeeze or dot some paint in the box. Close the lid. Roll and shake the marbles and paint around until the card has a design. Carefully take it out of the box and remove the masking tape. Let dry. Add stickers or a message to the front of the card where the masking tape left a blank area.

MAKING MERRY CARD

When you are making your own greeting cards, it is best to choose a design that you can make in multiples quickly. You'll love this "Merry" card that will keep you smiling while you make them by the dozens.

WHAT YOU NEED

Brown kraft blank cards and envelopes • Rubber stamp with desired greeting • Black ink pad • Pencil with new eraser • Fine gold glitter • Crafts glue • Paper punch • Narrow gold ribbon

WHAT YOU DO

1. Lay out the cards so you can work on more than one at a time. Use the rubber stamp to stamp the message on multiple cards. Let dry. Dip the eraser end of the pencil in crafts glue to make dots around the message. Dust with gold glitter. Repeat for all the cards. Let dry.

2. Punch a hole in the corner of the card and add a narrow gold ribbon if desired.

SHIMMERING SNOWFLAKES

For easy elegance, choose a gray-and-white color scheme with touches of silver. Layer satin ribbon, metallic eyelash trim, and snowflake ornaments on any size package, adjusting the number of bands to fit.

PRETTY IN PLAID

For a very small package, be bold with your ribbon and topper. If you're using flat ornaments or die-cut shapes, stack several sizes for dimension. When wrapping with plaids and stripes, position patterns on the diagonal for a completely different look. Narrow ribbons and festive cordings let the package tie-ons take center stage.

FABULOUS WOODLANDS

Create a mini woodland scene atop a metallic wood-grain paper. Use a greeting card for the background trees and snow, then hot-glue mini bottlebrush trees on top.

RED VELVET REINDEER

Trace the inside of a stencil onto flocked self-adhesive paper, cut it out, and adhere it to solid-color gift wrap for a quick and clever package.

WHAT YOU NEED

Stencil or an enlarged pattern of your choice • Self-adhesive flocked, suede, or velvet paper • Scissors or utility knife

WHAT YOU DO

1. Lay the stencil on self-adhesive flocked, suede, or velvet paper and trace around the inside of the design.
2. Cut out the shape. With many velvet or suede papers, you simply peel off the paper backing and apply the silhouette directly to your wrapping paper. Depending on the brand you choose, some flocked papers need to be ironed onto the paper. We recommend following the manufacturer's instructions for applying the paper.

PAINT BOIS FOR FUN

French for "false wood," the ancient technique of faux bois is as easy as it is beautiful. Purchase a graining tool at your paint shop or crafts store and pull it through wet acrylic crafts paint.

WHAT YOU NEED

Acrylic crafts paint • Liquitex glazing medium • Paper plate • Foam brush • Wood graining tool

WHAT YOU DO

1. Mix equal parts acrylic paint and glazing medium on a paper plate. The glaze slows down the drying time and gives you longer to work.
2. With a foam brush the same width as your graining tool, brush a line of the mixture onto your paper. Immediately go over the paint with the graining tool, dragging it downward through the paint mix and gently rocking your hand to create the knots. Brush on another line of paint and repeat until you cover the entire piece of paper.

A MATTER OF SPLATTER

With the flick of your wrist, release dots and drips of thinned paint from a paintbrush onto your paper. Make fewer dots for a light dusting of snow or more dots for a real blizzard!

WHAT YOU NEED

Paper plate • Acrylic crafts paint • Newspaper or drop cloth • Flat paintbrush or toothbrush • Paint stirrer, ruler, or similar

WHAT YOU DO

1. On a paper plate, dilute acrylic crafts paint with a little water so the paint is thinner and falls from the brush easily.
2. Splatters tend to travel, so start by protecting your work surface. To replicate the splatters shown here, use a flat 1-inch brush and dip it in diluted paint. Use a flick-of-the-wrist motion or tap brush onto stirrer or ruler to deposit droplets directly onto paper. Let drops dry thoroughly.
3. For an alternative method, choose an old toothbrush. Dip the bristles into thinned paint, aim the bristles toward the paper, and run your thumb across them to create a spray. Practice to perfect your aim.

COATED WITH TEXTURE

Dry-brush with a stiff-bristle brush and a small amount of paint to add texture. Dry-brushing is just what it suggests—you pick up a small amount of paint on the brush bristles and drag in one direction across the paper.

WHAT YOU NEED

Acrylic crafts paint • Paper plate • Chip brush or paintbrush • Paper towels

WHAT YOU DO

1. With a small amount of paint on a paper plate, dip the bristles of the brush into the paint and wipe off most of the paint on a paper towel. Lightly drag color on the paper, working in one direction, until you are pleased with the amount of coverage.
2. If you want to apply paint in both directions to create a crosshatch or loose plaid pattern, let the first layer dry, then turn your paper 90 degrees and apply paint. Keep the dry-brushing light so you can stamp or stencil other motifs over the top to coordinate with other papers.

Using simple painting techniques such as graining, splatter painting, or dry-brushing creates unique wrapping papers that are easy to make and so beautiful.

Visions of Sugarplums

Bring clever crafted versions of confections and some sugar and spice into your holiday home for the sweetest Christmas ever.

LOLLIPOP WREATH

Greet your holiday guests with a fresh evergreen wreath studded with lollipops in all shapes and sizes. Simply wire the little treasures first and then wire them into the wreath. Add a big striped bow at the top and your front door will say "Merry Christmas!" in the sweetest of ways.

GUMDROP CENTERPIECE

Sugary gumdrops and sweet-swirl lollipops combine to create a quick-to-make centerpiece for your holiday table.

WHAT YOU NEED

Square glass vase • Jar small enough to fit inside the vase • Gumdrops • Skewer • Large lollipops • Sprigs of fresh evergreen

WHAT YOU DO

1. Be sure the vase and jar are clean and dry. Place the jar inside the vase. While holding the inside jar, carefully drop the gumdrops around it, filling the space between the two pieces. Use a skewer to poke the gumdrops around to desired areas.

2. Place the lollipops in the jar. Add the sprigs of evergreen.

CANDYLAND TREE
Faux candies of all kinds bring this sweet tree to life.

FELT SWIRL CANDY

WHAT YOU NEED

Nonwoven felt such as National Nonwovens in desired colors • Hot-glue gun and glue sticks • Embroidery needle • Embroidery floss

WHAT YOU DO

1. Cut three 1×12-inch strips from assorted colors of felt. Stack strips so they're staggered by ⅛ inch at one short end. (Staggering makes the candy shape easier to roll.) Secure with a dot of hot glue under each layer at staggered end.
2. Starting at glued end, tightly roll felt layers to create a swirl, gluing as needed. Trim to even ends. Secure with hot glue.
3. Cut two 1×2-inch pieces from one color felt. Cut a notch in one 1-inch edge of each piece. At the other 1-inch edge, cut a ½-inch slit. Overlap the resulting tabs to form a small cup in the felt, creating roughly a 90-degree angle. Secure with hot glue.
4. Hot-glue the flat outer side of cupped edge to the side of swirl; glue other cupped strip to opposite side of swirl.
5. Thread an embroidery needle with embroidery floss. Push needle through ornament from bottom to top. Leaving a loop for hanging, push needle back through to bottom; knot floss.

FELT RIBBON CANDY

WHAT YOU NEED

Felt in assorted colors • Hot-glue gun and glue sticks • Embroidery needle • Embroidery floss

WHAT YOU DO

1. Cut a 1¼×12-inch felt strip from two shades of felt. Layer strips and secure with a dot of hot glue at one end.
2. To create even loops, lay a pencil across the felt layers 1½ inches from glue end. Fold layers over pencil to create a small loop (Photo 1). Secure loop with a dot of hot glue; remove pencil.
3. Repeat, alternating directions to the end of strip (Photo 2). Trim end.
4. Thread an embroidery needle with embroidery floss. Push needle through ornament from bottom to top. Leaving a loop for hanging, push needle back through to bottom; knot floss.

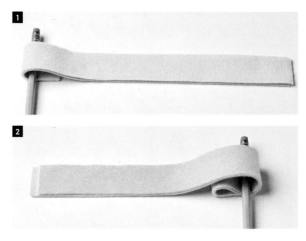

CREPE PAPER CANDY

WHAT YOU NEED

Sheet of crepe paper • 1-inch foam ball • Hot-glue gun and glue sticks • Narrow ribbon

WHAT YOU DO

1. Cut a 5×6-inch piece of crepe paper. Lay foam ball in center. Roll crepe paper around ball. Hot-glue edge to secure.
2. Pinch and twist both ends next to ball. Secure twisted ends with ribbon.

SIMPLY SWEET GARLANDS

Nothing could be sweeter, or easier, than making strings of candy garlands for your mantel or tree. Choose candies in colors that suit your holiday theme.

WHAT YOU NEED

Soft candies such as gumdrops • Dental floss • Needle for threading • Warm water • Paper towel • Velveteen ribbon in hues to complement candy • Scissors

WHAT YOU DO

On a clean surface, lay the candies out to plan the design. Cut the desired length of floss and thread the needle. Thread the candies onto the floss, dipping the needle into warm water when needed to clean the needle (for easier threading). Tie a piece of ribbon between the candies and trim the ends. Double-loop the thread at each end to secure the candies on the floss.

CANDY COATINGS

Dip inexpensive frosted glass balls for a sweet richness that's different every time. A diluted glue and food coloring mix is the secret to the rainbow colors. To dry without smudges or mess, hang wet ornaments on wooden skewers set across the top of an empty box. For a two-color design, make sure the first color is dry before you dip the ornament a second time.

SPRINKLE WRAPS

Little bits of confetti made from paper are sprinkled over a simple white wrap to dress it up for the holidays.

WHAT YOU NEED

Cardstock in various colors • Sprinkle-shape punch, see Sources, page 160 (optional) • White kraft paper • Spray adhesive • White tissue paper

WHAT YOU DO

Punch sprinkle shapes from cardstock if using a punch. If cutting your own, cut small rectangle shapes and place in a small container for ease in handling. Wrap gift in white kraft paper. Spray the top of the package with spray adhesive and sprinkle on the sprinkles. When dry, wrap the gift with white tissue paper.

CANDY ART ORNAMENTS

Candy-color felt is cut into shapes and layered together to create pieces of art to hang on your tree or dress up a package.

WHAT YOU NEED

Nonwoven felt such as National Nonwovens in desired colors • Hot-glue gun and glue sticks • Embroidery thread • Polyester fiberfill • Ribbon for hanging

WHAT YOU DO

FOR EACH ORNAMENT

Cut two 4-inch circles from desired color of felt for each ornament. See page 158 for Stitch Diagrams.

TO MAKE THE STRIPED ORNAMENT

Cut ½-inch and ¼-inch strips. Use hot glue to adhere onto front circle shape; trim excess. Lay on top of plain circle and sew with embroidery thread around the outside using a Blanket Stitch, attaching ribbon to hang in the middle of the two layers. Before the perimeter is fully stitched, fill with polyfill. Continue stitching until closed.

TO MAKE THE PINWHEEL ORNAMENT

1. Cut 5 shapes using the template, below. Attach to one of the circles using hot glue.

2. Stack one plain circle and one circle with pinwheel design. Sew with embroidery thread around the outside using a Blanket Stitch, attaching ribbon to hang in the middle of the two layers. Before the perimeter is fully stitched, fill with polyfill. Continue stitching until closed.

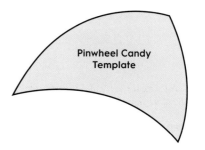

Pinwheel Candy
Template

SPRINKLE-FILLED BALLS

Clear glass balls become little vessels to hold hundreds of colorful sprinkles to add to packages or hang on the tree. Simply remove the top of the ornament and use a funnel to fill. Tie a ribbon through the top and hang or tie to a box. For a special gift, bake some cookies and decorate with the same type of sprinkles.

CANDY LEAF WREATH

Welcome your sweet-tooth guests with this sugar-dusted wreath made from leaf-shape gumdrops.

WHAT YOU NEED

Flat wreath form • Leaf-shape gumdrop candies, see Sources, page 160 • Red gumdrops • Hot-glue gun and glue sticks

WHAT YOU DO

Lay the wreath form on a flat surface and plan the design. Starting at the top, use hot glue to adhere the gumdrops to the wreath form, working in small sections at a time. Cut gumdrops in half or quarters to fit in small areas. Let dry. Loop a ribbon around the top for hanging.

Easy Nibbles and Sips

Serve a few of these savory starters and holiday drinks as a prelude to dinner or feature as an appetizer buffet.

NACHO CHICKEN DRUMMETTES

Be sure to set out a stack of napkins with these crunchy-coated drummies.

WHAT YOU NEED

1½ cups mild taco sauce
4   cups crushed tortilla chips
3   lb. chicken drummettes or 12 chicken drumsticks
     Shredded Mexican cheese blend (optional)
     Desired dipping sauce(s), such as bottled ranch salad dressing, salsa, mild taco sauce, and/or barbecue sauce (optional)

WHAT YOU DO

1. Preheat oven to 400°F. Line a 15×10-inch baking pan with foil. Grease foil; set pan aside. Pour the 1½ cups taco sauce into a shallow dish. Place tortilla chips in another shallow dish. Dip chicken into taco sauce, then into tortilla chips, turning to coat. Place chicken in the prepared baking pan.
2. Bake 30 to 40 minutes or until chicken is no longer pink (175°F for drumsticks). Do not turn chicken while baking. If desired, sprinkle with cheese and serve with desired dipping sauce(s). Makes 6 servings.

CHICKEN-CHORIZO MEATBALLS

This recipe puts a new spin on homemade meatballs by using ground chicken and chorizo sausage for a little extra kick.

WHAT YOU NEED

2   eggs, lightly beaten
½   cup fine dry bread crumbs
½   cup finely chopped onion
¼   cup milk
½   tsp. salt
½   tsp. black pepper
1   lb. ground chicken
1   14- to 15-oz. pkg. uncooked chorizo sausage
1   cup salsa verde
¾   cup finely chopped fresh poblano pepper*
¼   cup chicken broth
2   cloves garlic, minced
1   tsp. ground cumin

WHAT YOU DO

1. Preheat oven to 375°F. Line a 15×10-inch baking pan with foil. In a large bowl combine first six ingredients (through black pepper). Add ground chicken and sausage; mix well. Shape into 36 meatballs and place in prepared pan. Bake 25 to 30 minutes or until meatballs are cooked through (165°F). Drain off fat.
2. Transfer meatballs to a 3½- or 4-qt. slow cooker. For sauce, in a small bowl stir together remaining ingredients; pour over meatballs.

3. Cover and cook on low 3 to 4 hours or high 1½ to 2 hours. Serve immediately or keep warm, covered, on warm or low up to 2 hours. Makes 36 servings.
*Tip Chile peppers contain oils that can irritate your skin and eyes. Wear plastic or rubber gloves when working with them.

BABA GANOUSH

This rich Mediterranean eggplant spread is great for slathering on fresh veggies or toasted baguette slices.

WHAT YOU NEED

3	1-lb. eggplants
½	cup tahini (sesame seed paste)
¼	cup fresh flat-leaf parsley leaves
¼	cup lemon juice
2	cloves garlic
1	tsp. kosher salt
1	Tbsp. olive oil
	Crushed red pepper (optional)
	Assorted dippers

WHAT YOU DO

1. Preheat oven to 425°F. Line a 15×10-inch baking pan with foil. Prick eggplants all over with a fork. Place in prepared pan. Roast 30 to 40 minutes or until very soft and skin is charred. Cool until easy to handle.

2. Remove and discard skins from eggplants. In a food processor or blender combine eggplant pulp, tahini, parsley, lemon juice, garlic, and salt. Cover and pulse until nearly smooth, leaving some pieces of eggplant. Season to taste with additional salt.

3. Transfer dip to a serving bowl. Drizzle with oil and, if desired, sprinkle with crushed red pepper. Serve with dippers. Makes 18 servings.

HUMMUS

About 15 minutes start to finish, hummus is always a favorite at parties.

WHAT YOU NEED

1	15-oz. can no-salt-added chickpeas, rinsed and drained
2	Tbsp. lemon juice
2	Tbsp. tahini (sesame seed paste)
2	cloves garlic, minced
¾	tsp. salt
3	Tbsp. olive oil
1	Tbsp. water
	Black pepper
	Assorted dippers

WHAT YOU DO

1. In a food processor or blender combine first five ingredients (through salt). Cover and process or blend until smooth. With machine running, add oil and the water in thin, steady streams until mixture is smooth. Season to taste with pepper and additional salt. Transfer hummus to a serving bowl. If desired, drizzle with additional oil and sprinkle with additional pepper. Serve with dippers. Makes 14 servings.

Variations If desired, stir in one or more of the following or use as a topping: ⅓ cup crumbled feta cheese, chopped pitted ripe olives or kalamata olives, or chopped roasted red bell peppers; ¼ cup sliced green onions or basil pesto; and/or 1 Tbsp. chopped fresh dill.

MARINATED MOZZARELLA WITH BASIL

Instead of using fresh mozzarella for this appetizer, try another fresh soft cheese, such as queso fresco or feta.

WHAT YOU NEED

¼   cup fresh basil leaves
¼   cup olive oil
1   tsp. coarse ground black pepper
1   to 2 tsp. balsamic vinegar
1   lb. fresh mozzarella cheese, cut into 1-inch cubes
    Tomato slices (optional)
    Crackers or baguette slices

WHAT YOU DO

1. Set aside several whole basil leaves. Using a sharp knife, chop the remaining basil leaves. In a medium bowl combine chopped basil, oil, pepper, and vinegar. Add cheese cubes to herb-oil mixture, tossing gently until cheese is well-coated. Cover and chill at least 1 hour or up to 5 days.

2. Transfer cheese mixture to a serving dish; top with the reserved whole basil leaves and, if desired, tomato slices. Serve with crackers or baguette slices. Makes 14 servings.

TEX-MEX CHEESE DIP

Plan to double this recipe for a crowd because this addicting cheesy dip is going disappear fast. Go the extra mile and top with pickled jalapeños and/or additional beans and corn.

WHAT YOU NEED
1   8-oz. pkg. cream cheese, cut up
½   cup sour cream
½   cup mayonnaise
1   cup shredded Monterey Jack cheese with jalapeño peppers (4 oz.)
1   Tbsp. taco seasoning or 2 tsp. chili powder
1   cup canned black beans, rinsed and drained
1   cup frozen corn, thawed
1   4-oz. can diced green chile peppers, drained, or 2 Tbsp. finely chopped pickled jalapeño peppers
    Assorted dippers

WHAT YOU DO
1. In a medium saucepan stir together cream cheese, sour cream, and mayonnaise. Stir in shredded cheese and taco seasoning.
2. Cook and stir over medium-low heat until mixture is melted and smooth. Stir in beans, corn, and chile peppers; heat through. Serve with dippers. Makes 14 servings.
Tip If you're not serving this dip immediately (or toting it to a party), transfer to a 1½-qt. slow cooker. Keep warm, covered, on warm or low up to 2 hours, stirring occasionally.

BROWN BUTTER CAULIFLOWER ARTICHOKE DIP

This creamy dip is packed with cauliflower florets, artichokes, and hazelnuts, and it's delicious when spread on hearty crackers or fresh vegetables.

WHAT YOU NEED
2   14-oz. cans artichoke hearts, rinsed and drained
¼   cup butter
2   cups small cauliflower florets
1   clove garlic, minced
1   8-oz. carton sour cream
2   Tbsp. all-purpose flour
½   cup mayonnaise
¾   cup finely shredded Parmesan cheese
¼   cup hazelnuts, toasted and coarsely chopped
2   Tbsp. chopped fresh sage leaves
    Crackers and/or sliced fresh vegetables

WHAT YOU DO
1. Preheat oven to 350°F. Place artichoke hearts in a fine mesh sieve or colander. To remove excess liquid, firmly press on artichoke hearts with paper towels. Chop artichoke hearts. Set aside.

2. In a large skillet melt butter over medium-high heat. Continue cooking 1 to 2 minutes or until butter just starts to brown. Add cauliflower and garlic. Cook and stir 4 minutes or until cauliflower is golden brown. Remove from heat; cool slightly. Set aside ½ cup cauliflower mixture.
3. In a large bowl stir together sour cream and flour until combined. Stir in mayonnaise, ½ cup of the Parmesan cheese, artichokes, remaining cauliflower mixture, 2 Tbsp. of the hazelnuts, and 1 Tbsp. of the chopped sage. Transfer to a 9-inch pie plate. Sprinkle with remaining cheese and reserved ½ cup cauliflower.
4. Bake, uncovered, 30 minutes or until edges are lightly browned and mixture is bubbly. Cool 15 minutes. Top with remaining hazelnuts and sage leaves. Makes 16 servings.

BEER-CHEESE FONDUE

This easy appetizer will be the first to disappear at any gathering. The slow cooker will keep the fondue warm and smooth while your guests nibble and nosh.

WHAT YOU NEED

1½ cups reduced-sodium chicken broth
1¼ cups heavy cream
½ cup lager beer
2 cloves garlic, minced
½ cup butter, softened
½ cup all-purpose flour
1½ tsp. spicy brown mustard
2 cups shredded mild cheddar cheese (8 oz.)
1 cup shredded sharp cheddar cheese (4 oz.)
Assorted dippers, such as French bread cubes, soft pretzels, and cut vegetables

WHAT YOU DO

1. In a 1½- or 2-qt. slow cooker combine the broth, cream, beer, and garlic. Cover and cook on low 4 to 5 hours.
2. Turn cooker to high. In a bowl stir together butter and flour until a paste forms; whisk paste into broth mixture until smooth (mixture will thicken immediately). Cover and cook 30 minutes more.
3. Whisk mustard into broth mixture. Gradually whisk in both cheeses until smooth. Serve with dippers. Makes 22 servings.
Stove-Top Directions In a medium saucepan melt butter over medium heat. Add garlic; cook and stir 2 minutes. Whisk in flour; cook and stir 1 minute. Gradually whisk in broth, cream, and beer. Cook and stir until thickened and bubbly. Whisk in the mustard until smooth, then gradually whisk in cheeses until melted and smooth. If desired for serving, transfer fondue to a slow cooker set to warm.

ROSEMARY PECAN SNACK MIX

A flavorful blend of nuts, crunchy crackers, Parmesan cheese, and herbs, makes for an irresistible crowd-pleasing appetizer.

WHAT YOU NEED

3	cups pecan halves
2	cups oyster crackers
2	cups white cheddar cheese crackers
1	cup pumpkin seeds (pepitas)
1½	cups freshly grated Parmesan cheese
2	Tbsp. packed brown sugar
2	Tbsp. chopped fresh rosemary
2	tsp. crushed red pepper
4	cloves garlic, minced
½	cup butter, melted

WHAT YOU DO

1. Preheat oven to 300°F. Line a 15×10-inch baking pan with parchment paper or foil.

2. In a large bowl combine pecans, oyster crackers, cheese crackers, and pumpkin seeds. Add Parmesan, brown sugar, rosemary, crushed red pepper, and garlic; toss to combine. Pour melted butter over combined ingredients and toss gently to coat.

3. Spread the mix on the prepared baking pan in an even layer. Bake 30 minutes, stirring once halfway through.

4. Let cool on a wire rack. Store leftovers in an airtight container up to 1 week. Makes 21 servings.

CHEESY SNACK MIX

What's not to love? This snack mix has it all—crispy, salty, and cheesy. It's also a good choice for individual gift bags for neighbors and friends.

WHAT YOU NEED

4	cups crispy corn and rice cereal
1	1.75-oz. can shoestring potatoes
2	cups crisp breadsticks, broken into 2-inch pieces
2	cups bite-size cheese crackers
1	6-oz. can smoke-flavor whole almonds (optional)
¼	cup butter or margarine
3	Tbsp. bottled clear Italian salad dressing
¼	cup grated Parmesan cheese
¼	tsp. garlic powder

WHAT YOU DO

1. Preheat oven to 300°F. In a 15×10-inch baking pan combine cereal, shoestring potatoes, breadsticks, cheese crackers, and, if desired, almonds.

2. In a saucepan combine butter and salad dressing. Heat over low until butter is melted. Stir in Parmesan cheese and garlic powder. Drizzle butter mixture over cereal mixture; toss gently to coat.

3. Bake 30 minutes, stirring twice. Spread snack mix on a large sheet of foil; let cool. Makes 18 servings.

SPARKLING STRAWBERRY MIMOSA

Give your mimosa a twist with muddled strawberries and a drizzle of maple syrup.

WHAT YOU NEED

4   cups strawberries, hulled and quartered
4   oranges, peeled and sectioned
1   750-milliliter bottle champagne or sparkling apple juice, chilled
    Ice cubes
    Maple syrup (optional)

WHAT YOU DO

In a large pitcher combine strawberries and oranges. Muddle with a wooden spoon. Stir in champagne. Serve over ice. Drizzle with maple syrup, if desired. Makes 6 servings.

GOLDEN WASSAIL

Classic holiday punch gets a family-friendly spin in this juice-based, alcohol-free drink recipe. (Pictured on page 119.)

WHAT YOU NEED

4   cups unsweetened pineapple juice
4   cups apple cider or apple juice
1½   cups apricot nectar
1   cup orange juice
2   3-inch sticks cinnamon
1   tsp. whole cloves
¼   tsp. whole cardamom seeds, crushed
     Gold luster dust (optional)
     Apple slices (optional)

WHAT YOU DO

1. In a large saucepan combine all ingredients. Bring to boiling; reduce heat. Simmer, uncovered, 15 minutes. Strain; discard cloves and cardamom.
2. If desired, decorate bowl by wetting rim and brushing with gold luster dust. Transfer punch to bowl. If desired, garnish with additional cinnamon sticks and apple slices. Makes 10 servings.

HOT SPICED APPLE CIDER

To spike this aromatic hot cider, add 1 oz. Calvados, apple brandy, or brandy to each serving.

WHAT YOU NEED

2   3-inch cinnamon sticks
4   whole cloves
4   whole allspice
8   cups apple cider
¼   cup fresh lemon juice
     Calvados, apple brandy, or brandy (optional)
     Freshly grated nutmeg (optional)
     Apple slices

WHAT YOU DO

1. For spice bag, place cinnamon, cloves, and allspice on double-thick 6-inch square of 100%-cotton cheesecloth. Bring up corners; tie closed with 100% cotton kitchen string.
2. In a 4-qt. Dutch oven combine cider, lemon juice, and spice bag. Bring to a simmer (do not boil). Reduce heat and simmer, uncovered, 20 minutes. Remove spice bag.
3. To serve, ladle hot cider into 6-oz. mugs. Add 2 Tbsp. Calvados to each mug if desired. Top with nutmeg, if desired, and apple slices. Makes 10 servings.
Slow Cooker variation Prepare as directed in a 4-qt. slow cooker. Cover and cook on low 2 to 3 hours. Remove spice bag and serve as directed.
Hot Pomegranate Cider Prepare as directed, except reduce apple cider to 6 cups and add 2 cups pomegranate juice and 2 Tbsp. grenadine. Substitute pomegranate liqueur for the Calvados (if using). Serve with pomegranate seeds.
Earl Grey Cider Toddy Prepare as directed, except reduce cider to 6 cups and add 2 cups water. Substitute tangerine or orange juice for the lemon juice and omit cinnamon sticks, cloves, and allspice. After simmering, remove from heat and add 4 Earl Grey tea bags; let stand 10 minutes. Remove tea bags. Serve with strips of orange zest.
Honeyed Hot Cider Sauvignon Prepare as directed, except reduce cider to 4 cups and add one 750 ml bottle of Sauvignon Blanc or other dry white wine and ½ cup honey. Substitute regular brandy for the Calvados (if using).
Hot Apple Pie Cider Prepare as directed, except stir in 2 tsp. vanilla after simmering, and substitute bourbon for the Calvados (if using). Top with whipped cream and shortbread cookie crumbs.

GIN SHRUB FIZZ

A shrub is a non-alcoholic syrup made of a combination of concentrated fruits, aromatics, sugar, and vinegar. This sweet, yet acidic mixer is enjoyed as a component of a mixed drink with club soda.

WHAT YOU NEED

3   **lemons**
3   **16-oz. pkg. frozen unsweetened blackberries or 12 cups fresh blackberries**
2   **cups sugar**
2   **cups white balsamic vinegar**
½   **cup fresh sage leaves**
1   **Tbsp. gin (½ oz.)**
    Ice
3   **Tbsp. club soda (1½ oz.)**
    Lime wedge

WHAT YOU DO

1. For the blackberry and sage shrub syrup, remove 1 Tbsp. zest and squeeze ½ cup juice from lemons. In a 3½- or 4-qt. slow cooker combine lemon zest and juice, blackberries, sugar, and vinegar. Cover and cook on low 4 hours. Stir in sage. Let stand, uncovered, 1 hour.
2. Press berry mixture through a fine-mesh sieve; discard solids. Store, covered, in the refrigerator up to 3 months. Makes about 6 cups syrup.
3. For a Gin Shrub Fizz, pour ¼ cup (2 oz.) blackberry and sage shrub syrup into an ice-filled glass. Slowly pour in ¾ cup (6 oz.) club soda; stir gently. Serve with a lime wedge. Makes 1 serving.
Shrub Mimosa Pour 2 Tbsp. (1 oz.) blackberry and sage shrub syrup into a chilled champagne flute. Slowly fill with 6 Tbsp. (3 oz.) Prosecco; stir gently.

Gather Together...

Perfect Place Settings

Make your Christmas table the center of attention with place settings that bring smiles and happy anticipation.

GOLD RUSH

The fresh energy of natural green glows when partnered with gold. A shimmery mat hosts unmatched plates of delicate green motifs grounded on a gold, linen-texture glass charger. An embroidered green vine lines the edge of a napkin tied with a simple white cord knotted around a sprig of eucalyptus. The fresh green repeats on stems that weave among an array of mismatched brass candlesticks.

Never leave a burning candle unattended.

STRAW POWER

There's nothing flat about the paper in this ensemble. Dinnerware—a combination of solid-color and patterned plates—sings atop a wood charger and a place mat filled with musical notes. Wood-style straws cut and formed into snowflake-shape ornaments mingle among a forest of paper trees made from musical note scrapbook paper. Wood flatware handles support the natural spirit.

PERFECTLY PLAID

The pulse of Christmas always beats with plaid. A velvet place mat with a silk border sets the tone for plates featuring variations of the structured pattern. A nod to Scotland, where tartan first made its mark, comes a kilt pin that adorns the velvet-trimmed napkin. Buffalo plaid in red and black stretches under the centerpiece trimmings of winter greens, pinecones, and cardinals.

HOLIDAY FASHION

Like a little black dress on a holiday partygoer, black lends a chic vibe to a modern setting. A striped, round place mat circles plates festooned with a dot motif. Their matte finish is repeated on gunmetal-color flatware. Edged in silver, a black napkin is secured with a fashion-forward bow made of striped grosgrain ribbon topped with a sparkling jewel. A tray of silver and gold dazzles with chic black candles and red bows.

Never leave a burning candle unattended.

PERFECT PEARINGS

There's no doubt that roses bring a touch of elegance to any scene. Here, the velvety white blooms mingle with seasonal pears, fragrant eucalyptus, and silver sleigh bells for a sophisticated setting. A gold charger lends refinement to a simple white plate topped with a cleverly folded napkin and a green pear bearing a silver-scripted place card.

TO MAKE FOLDED NAPKIN

Who doesn't delight in a fancy, folded napkin? Lay your napkin flat and fold each corner into the center. Flip it over and repeat to create a nest for the fruit. To make the personalized name tags, snip real or paper eucalyptus leaves and script guests' names in silver paint pen. Tie tags to the fruit stem with an ultra-thin satin ribbon.

INTO THE WOODS

Douglas, Fraser, balsam. No matter what type of fir you prefer, this felt one is sure to be a sensation at your next holiday dinner party. As a handcrafted accent on your tabletop, the tree looks striking atop a white plate and silver charger while serving as a cradle for hammered-silver utensils. Each setting is enhanced with a red plaid napkin and an arrangement of pinecones and fresh-cut fir.

TO MAKE FELT ACCENT

Make your own pattern to nestle silverware by tracing a tree shape (search online or coloring books for easy-to-draw outlines) and enlarging it to the height of your plate's diameter using a copy machine. Cut out the paper tree and trace the shape onto a piece of felt, then cut out the felt tree with sharp scissors. Use a ruler and crafts knife to add slits for the silverware.

DINNER MUSIC

Your guests may be encouraged to break out in song when classic Christmas carols are the party theme. Photocopy the chorus of old favorites from a songbook and use as place mats. Consider a different song for each setting to stir memories and conversation. Pillar candles stacked on cut birch rounds are wrapped with more music and tied with twine to continue the harmonious theme.

Never leave a burning candle unattended.

THE GOLD STANDARD

Everything looks a little more luxurious when touched with gold. Paired with a fluted ruby-red dinner plate, polka-dot accent plate, and red napkins, these gilded tabletop touches set a new standard of elegance. Let your guests know just how welcome they are with a rich ensemble that includes a take-home gift box tied with a red velvet ribbon. They'll think you have a heart of gold.

TO MAKE NAPKIN PLACE SETTING

Super simple yet delightfully welcoming, this red napkin wrapped in ribbon looks as pretty as a package under the tree. All it takes is two folds and a thin ribbon. Tie the ribbon around the folded fabric as you would a package, and loop in a white gift tag for a place card.

CHRISTMAS VILLAGE

There's something alluring about miniature illuminated villages at Christmastime. Capture the magic of the centuries-old Putz house tradition by creating your own tabletop township with purchased cardboard houses available online or at crafts stores. Lit with battery-operated votives and scattered among a forest of bottle brush trees and fir clippings sprayed with faux snow, the scene is lively enough that you can almost hear tiny bells ringing.

Little Drummer Boy...
Oh What Fun!

Gather the entire family around the kitchen table for some crafting fun and holiday memories.

SPELL OUT CHRISTMAS TRIMS

Iron-on patch letters become easy-to-make ornaments with a few colorful add-ons.

WHAT YOU NEED

Iron-on letter patches • Nonwoven felts such as National Nonwovens in desired colors • Bakers twine • Iron • Scissors • Hot-glue gun and glue sticks • Mini pom-poms

WHAT YOU DO

1. Lay the patches on a piece of felt about the same size as the patch. Lay a looped piece of bakers twine between the two pieces for hanging. Using an iron, and following manufacturer's instructions, attach the patches to the felt.
2. When cooled, use scissors to trim around the perimeter of the letter. Attach mini pom-poms on the front with hot glue.

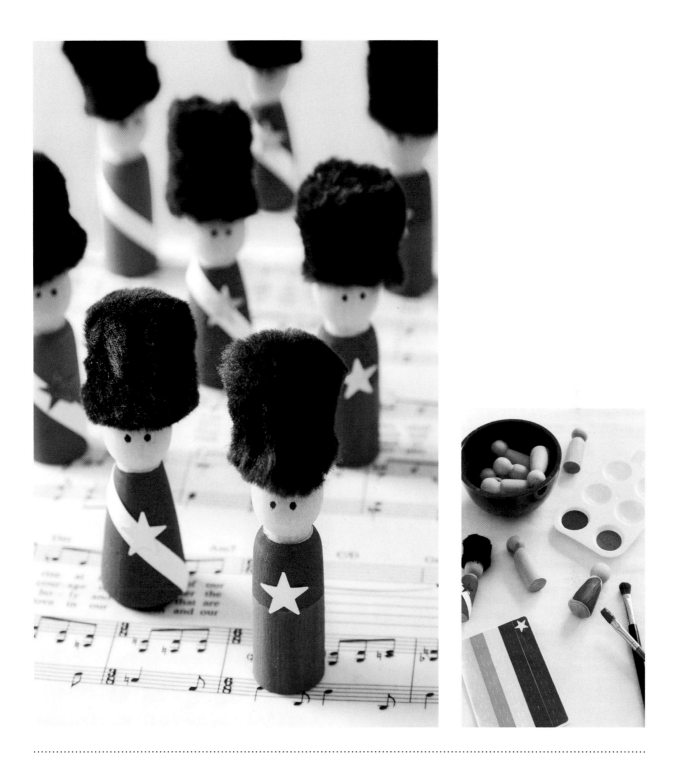

LITTLE DRUMMER BOYS

Wooden peg dolls come to life with just a little paint, a pom-pom, and shiny star stickers.

WHAT YOU NEED

Wooden peg dolls, see Sources, page 160 • Red and blue crafts paint • White card stock (optional) • Painters tape • Large black pom-poms • Scissors • Black permanent marker • Hot-glue gun and glue sticks • Star stickers

WHAT YOU DO

1. Place the wooden peg dolls on a covered surface. Paint the body of the figurines as desired, using painters tape to aid in any straight lines. Let dry.

2. To create the hats, trim around the sides of the black pom-pom until cylindrical shaped. Attach the hat and a small strip of white paper as a sash if desired. Attach star stickers. Make eyes with the black permanent marker.

SILLY REINDEER PUPPETS

The kids will have hours of fun making and playing with these colorful reindeer friends crafted from bright, fuzzy socks.

WHAT YOU NEED (FOR ONE PUPPET)

Colorful striped fuzzy sock • 2 ping pong balls • Black felt • Stiffened felt for antlers • Hot-glue gun and glue sticks • Pom-pom • Red or green felt

WHAT YOU DO

1. Lay the sock on a flat surface. Cut two small circles from black felt and attach to the ping pong balls with hot glue. Using the antler template, trace and cut two antlers from stiffened felt. Attach the antlers to the back of the ping pong balls with hot glue.

2. Using the ear template, trace and cut two ears from red or green felt. Fold each ear in half and secure with a dot of hot glue on one end. Using hot glue, attach ping pong balls to the fuzzy sock. When dry, attach ears slightly behind the ping pong balls. Attach the pom-pom for the nose.

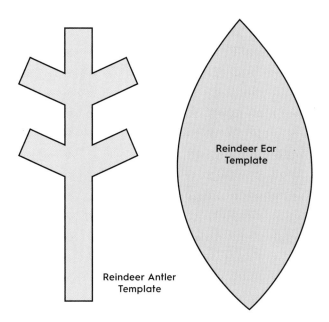

Reindeer Antler Template

Reindeer Ear Template

STAR POWER

Just like stitching string cards, these ornaments are easy and fun. Simply thread any type of yarn through the holes in wood cutouts to make stars in your favorite color schemes. Mix and match yarns of different shades, gauges, and textures. Raid your yarn stash for leftover yarns with knobby textures, metallic colors, or other jazzy accents.

WHAT YOU NEED

⅛-inch-thick wood cutouts in assorted shapes • Heavy-duty crafts punches • Yarn in assorted colors and weights • Yarn needle • Hot-glue gun and glue sticks (optional) • Felt pom-poms

WHAT YOU DO

1. Punch a large hole in the center of each wood shape using a heavy-duty crafts punch. Add smaller holes about ¼ inch from the edge, spacing holes evenly apart and staggering distance from edge if desired.
2. Thread yarn onto a yarn needle. Starting at back of ornament, loop yarn up through the center and down through an outer hole. Come up at center and down through another outer hole, working around the shape. If desired, thread one color yarn through every other hole then a second color in remaining holes to create a two-tone effect.
3. Knot or hot-glue yarn ends in back. Glue a felt pom-pom over the center hole. If desired, thread yarn through a top hole and knot together for a hanging loop.

CHRISTMAS FISHBOWL NIGHT LIGHT

It will be easier to sleep while waiting for Santa with happy fish sparkling in an easy-to-make night light.

WHAT YOU NEED

Fishbowl • Ornaments in shades of blue • Battery mini lights • Skewer • Scissors • White cardstock • Markers

WHAT YOU DO

1. Be sure the bowl is clean and dry. Arrange the blue ornaments and mini lights in the bowl, using the skewer to adjust as needed.

2. Trace the templates onto cardstock and cut out. Color with markers as desired. Slide the fish into the bowl along the flat side.

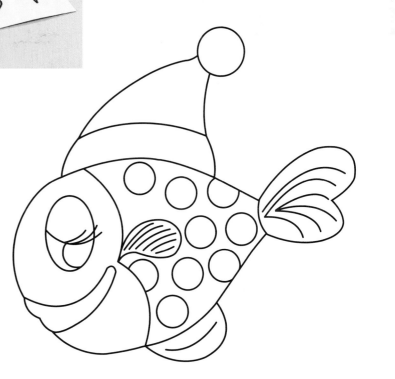

GIFTY ART BAGS

Drawings from children can be the best gift! Purchase plain cotton totes online (see Sources, page 160) and give the kids free reign to draw their favorite things. The cotton bags come in all kinds of sizes and shapes. Be sure each artist signs his or her work and then presents it to the lucky recipient.

YARN TREES

Gather the kids, and lots of colorful yarn and fabrics, and enjoy a creative, crafty snow day.

Kids can choose any colors of yarn to wrap these whimsical tabletop trees and then top them with homemade pom-poms.

WHAT YOU NEED

Foam cones, such as Styrofoam, in 9-inch and 12-inch heights ● Acrylic yarn in bright pink, bright green, bright blue, white ● Crafts glue ● Large pom-pom maker (optional)

WHAT YOU DO

1. Wrap desired color of yarn around a cone, starting at cone bottom and securing yarn with quick-setting glue as you work up the cone. When desired width of yarn is reached, trim yarn. Continue to wrap and glue yarn, working toward the point and switching yarn colors as desired.

2. If using a pom-pom maker, follow manufacturer's instructions to make a large white pom-pom. Or, make your own pom-pom using instructions on page 83. Trim long yarn tails and pom-pom yarns as needed. Apply glue to center of pom-pom and adhere to cone tip.

KIDS ART WRAPS

Instead of searching through rolls and rolls of holiday papers, choose some of your kid's favorite drawing creations and make copies to use as gift wrap. Choose one favorite image and surround it with ribbon, or use an all-over design as the main paper. Whatever you choose, everyone will cherish these personal wraps.

FABRIC AND FUN

A trip to the fabrics store, or an exploration through your scrap bin, lets kids customize these whimsical trees to their heart's content.

WHAT YOU NEED

1×12×36-inch sheet of foam, such as Styrofoam • Serrated knife or electric foam cutter • Foam balls, such as Styrofoam in 3-inch-diameter and 4-inch-diameter sizes • Assorted bright print fabrics • Crafts glue • Assorted ribbons • Decoupage medium, such as Mod Podge • Foam paintbrushes • Crystal glitter • 5⁄16-inch-diameter wooden dowel in 10-inch length (for tall tree) and two 8½-inch lengths (for short trees) • White acrylic paint

WHAT YOU DO

1. Trace triangle templates, below, onto white paper; cut out. Trace patterns onto foam sheet. Cut out the shapes using a serrated knife or electric foam cutter. Cut each foam ball in half.
2. Trace each triangle twice onto fabric. Cut out fabric shapes. Glue fabric to front and back of each triangle. Cut out ¾-inch-wide strips from fabric and glue to the triangle sides. Glue ribbon around bottom of each triangle.
3. Brush decoupage medium onto each ball half. While medium is still wet, sprinkle with glitter.
4. Paint dowels with white paint. Use a pencil to mark the center on bottom triangle edge. At the mark, push the pencil point through the fabric to make a hole. Dab glue onto one end of a dowel and insert the glued end into the hole. Dab glue onto opposite dowel end and push the dowel into the center of a ball half.

Large Tree
Enlarge 200%

Small Tree
Enlarge 200%

Medium Tree
Enlarge 200%

STITCHED WITH LOVE

Delight your little ones with a needlecraft tradition. Punch holes in simple cardstock shapes to outline the stitching patterns.

WHAT YOU NEED

White cardstock • Small hole punch • Large-eye embroidery needle • Acrylic yarn in red, teal, green

WHAT YOU DO

1. Enlarge and trace patterns onto white paper; cut out. Trace patterns onto white cardstock; cut out. Use a small hole punch to punch a hole at each circle.

2. Thread a large-eye embroidery needle with a long length of yarn, knot the yarn end and insert needle through a hole from back to front. Referring to the photo, opposite, and stitching diagrams below, stitch yarn from hole to hole to make desired design. Knot off yarn on back before starting a new yarn color.

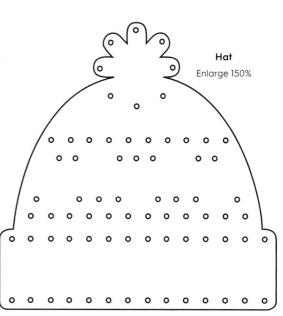

Hat
Enlarge 150%

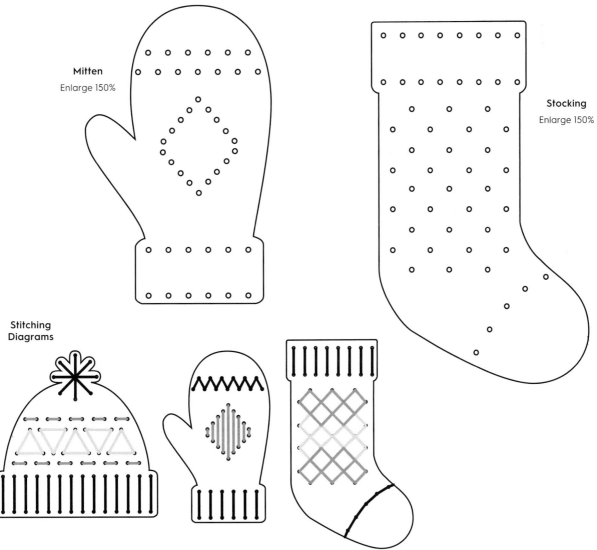

Mitten
Enlarge 150%

Stocking
Enlarge 150%

Stitching Diagrams

KITTY-KAT TABLE FAVOR

Make your holiday table complete with a sweet kitty favor that everyone will love!

WHAT YOU NEED

Nonwoven felt such as National Nonwovens in desired colors • Scissors • Paper punch • Crafts glue • Black ballpoint pen • Large sewing needle • Thin wire • Small candy canes • Small lollipop

WHAT YOU DO

1. Trace template pieces and cut out. Trace onto desired colors of felt and cut out. Use the paper punch to punch out eyes and foot pads. Referring to the photo and pattern, layer the pieces and glue in place except for the bow and feet/foot pads.

2. For whiskers, use a large sewing needle to punch a hole on one side of the face. Insert the end of the wire from front to back and pull across the back of the head to the opposite side. Punch another hole with the sewing needle and insert the wire through the hole so it comes out the front of the face. Adjust wire so it is even on both sides. Cut wire to desired length. Repeat for other whiskers.

3. Glue the two bow pieces together and glue onto the kitty's body at the neckline.

4. Cut two slits on the lower half of the kitty for the legs. Insert one foot through the slit and pull across the back to the opposite slit; insert the same foot into the second slit so it comes out to the front of the kitty. Pull just far enough that the two feet are equal on both sides. Glue foot pads in place.

5. Unwrap the candy cane and insert the straight end into the loop on the back of the kitty created by the feet. Add a small lollipop at the top.

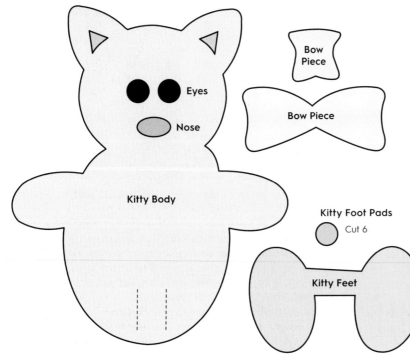

Angel Wings

Place on fold

EARTHY ANGELS

The kids will love to transform simple coffee filters and glitter into glorious angels complete with a magic halo.

WHAT YOU NEED

14 basket-style white coffee filters, 1- to 4-cup size • Silver glitter glue • Scissors • Crafts glue • White paper • 3½-inch-tall wooden peg doll (See Sources, page 160) • Metallic silver chenille pipe cleaner

WHAT YOU DO

1. For the skirt, flatten and stack two coffee filters. Run a line of glitter glue around the edge. Let dry.
2. Fold stacked filters in half. Accordion-pleat the half circle with 1-inch folds. Gently unfold the half-circle. Cut a 1-inch-diameter circle in the center of the filters. Slip the wooden peg doll through the opening in the filters. Glue the edge of the opening to the doll's neck, pleating as necessary for a snug fit. Fan out the skirt.
3. For the wings, trace the pattern, above, onto white paper and cut out. Layer two coffee filters and fold in half. Trace the pattern onto the folded filters, aligning the pattern with the fold as indicated on the pattern; cut out. Unfold wings. Run a line of glitter glue around all edges of top filter; let dry. Pinch wings at the center; secure pinched area with glue and glue wings to the back of the neck.
4. For the halo, bend the end of a short length of pipe cleaner into a small circle and twist end to secure. Put halo over the head and bend the straight portion around the neck, twisting at back to secure. Trim excess.

CRAZY FOR BEADS

Turn the fused-beads craze into a holiday decorating extravaganza. You can use purchased clear pegboard shapes, our template ideas, or create your own magical designs. No worries if the designs are not perfectly symmetrical—the end result will be playful and fun. String finished designs into ornaments, garlands, gift tags, and more.

WHAT YOU NEED

Fusible beads, such as Perler beads (See Sources, page 160) • Clear pegboard to fit design or generic pegboard (See Sources, page 160) • Fusible bead ironing paper or parchment paper • Iron • Bakers twine • Crafts glue

WHAT YOU DO

1. Choose the pattern you want to make. You can use templates that come from the bead manufacturer such as the star shown, below, you can use a plain purchased pegboard and create your own design using the patterns, right, or make your own design. See Sources, page 160 for bead and grid information.

2. Place the pegboard on a flat surface. Follow the pattern to place fusible beads onto the pegs until desired look is achieved.

3. Cover beads with ironing paper or parchment paper. Follow the manufacturer's instructions to press a warm, dry iron onto the paper and melt the beads just enough so they stick or fuse together.

4. Cool slightly. Remove paper and completed design from grid. Let cool completely.

5. Fold a length of bakers twine in half; slip through a hole or glue ends to back of ornament. Let dry.

STITCH DIAGRAMS

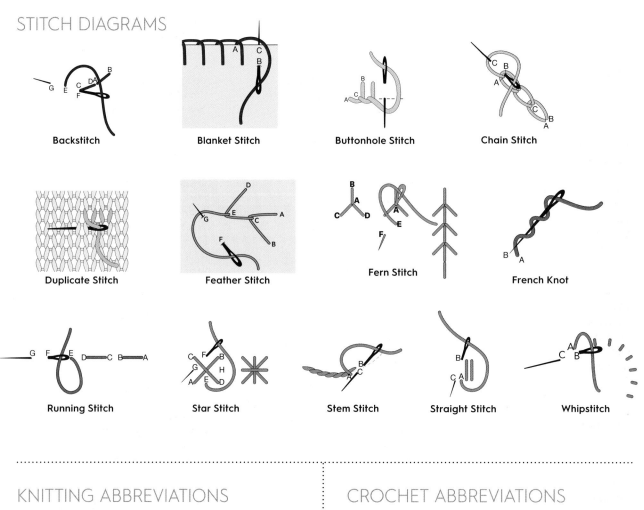

Backstitch	Blanket Stitch	Buttonhole Stitch	Chain Stitch
Duplicate Stitch	Feather Stitch	Fern Stitch	French Knot
Running Stitch	Star Stitch	Stem Stitch	Straight Stitch	Whipstitch

KNITTING ABBREVIATIONS

BEG begin(ning)
DEC decrease
INC increase
K knit
LP loop
M1 make one or to increase one
P purl
SSK slip, slip knit
TOG together

CROCHET ABBREVIATIONS

BEG begin(ning)
CH chain
DC double crochet
HDC half double crochet
INC increase
SC single crochet
SL ST slip stitch
ST(S stitch(es)

INDEX

A PROPER TABLE SETTING

When setting your dining table for the holidays, decide what dishes and flatware pieces are important for the meal you are serving. Use this guide to be sure your holiday table is beautifully set. The diagram shows where each piece should be placed. Adjust it as needed to fit your Christmas meal.

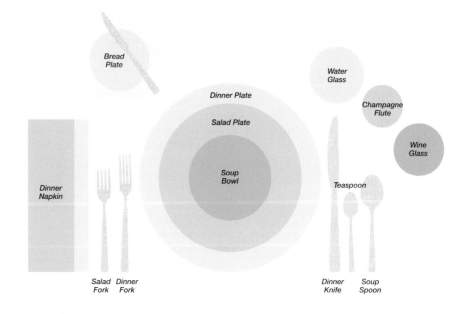

Bread Plate

Water Glass

Dinner Plate

Champagne Flute

Salad Plate

Wine Glass

Soup Bowl

Dinner Napkin

Teaspoon

Salad Fork   Dinner Fork

Dinner Knife   Soup Spoon

SOURCES

Bakers Twine
hobbylobby.com

Beads
Hilde & Joy/JoAnn's Fabrics
hobbylobby.com

Birch Bark
Natural Birch Bark/
   amazon.com

**Cardstock/Scrapbooking
   Supplies**
memoryboundscrapbookstore
   .com
hobbylobby.com

Crafts Paint
deltacreative.com

Cotton Totes
amazon.com

Felt
National Nonwovens
nationalnonwovens.com

Fuse Beads and Grids
fusebeadstore.com

Glass Domes
Collectingwarehouse.com

Glue
Aleene's Tacky Glue
aleenes.com

Leaf-Shaped Gumdrops
sweetgourmet.com

Papers and Stickers
memoryboundscrapbookstore
   .com
michaels.com

Paper Tape/Ribbon
hobbylobby.com
michaels.com

Paper-Wrapped Floral Stems
michaels.com

Pearl Cotton
Valdani.com

Ribbon
offray.com

Sprinkles Punch
MROCO
amazon.com

Wire Wreath Form
Sumind 4 Wire/amazon.com

Wood Embroidery Hoops
hobbylobby.com

Wood Ladybug Splits
Craft.wood.com

Wooden Peg Dolls
amazon.com

Wood Slices and Pieces
michaels.com
woodcrafter.com

Wool Pom-Poms
craftywoolfelt.com

Wrapping Papers
Society6.com
michaels.com

Wreath Moss
michaels.com

Yarn
yarnspirations.com
hobbylobby.com

CRAFT DESIGNERS

Ana Alvarez • Claire Bailey • Grace Bailey • Judy Bailey • Melissa Belanger • Henry Burnley • Noah Burnley • Carol Field Dahlstrom • Roger H. Dahlstrom • Lillian Dahlstrom • Elaine Koonce • Kylie Kurth (poems) • Kim Hutchinson • Pam Koelling • Christin Morgan • Iryna Morozova • Matthew Mead • Jennifer Peterson (gingerbread cookies) • Janet Pittman • Suzonne Stirling • Karla Taverna • Jan Temeyer • Roxie and Joe Wood • Patricia Welch • Svetlana Zabelina